Becoming a Metacognitive Teacher

A Guide for Early and Preservice Teachers

Roya Q. Scales
Thomas DeVere Wolsey
Seth A. Parsons

FOREWORD BY GERALD G. DUFFY

TEACHERS COLLEGE PRESS
TEACHERS COLLEGE | COLUMBIA UNIVERSITY
NEW YORK AND LONDON

Published by Teachers College Press,® 1234 Amsterdam Avenue, New York, NY 10027

Cover art by Emily Blankenship.

ILA Standards in Figure 3.3 used with permission of the International Literacy Association.

Engeström's Activity Theory triangle in Figure 3.4: Reproduced with permission of The Licensor through PLSclear, From Engeström, Y. (2015). *Learning by expanding: An activity-theoretical approach to developmental research* (2nd ed.). Cambridge, United Kingdom: Cambridge University Press.

Library of Congress Cataloging-in-Publication Data

Names: Scales, Roya Q., author. | Wolsey, Thomas DeVere, author. | Parsons, Seth A., author.
Title: Becoming a metacognitive teacher : a guide for early and preservice teachers / Roya Q. Scales, Thomas DeVere Wolsey, Seth A. Parsons ; foreword by Gerald G. Duffy.
Description: New York, NY : Teachers College Press, 2020. | Includes bibliographical references and index.
Identifiers: LCCN 2020007869 | ISBN 9780807764077 (hardback) | ISBN 9780807764060 (paperback) | ISBN 9780807778654 (epub)
Subjects: LCSH: Reflective teaching. | Teaching—Evaluation. | First year teachers. | Student teachers. | Metacognition.
Classification: LCC LB1025.3 .S297 2020 | DDC 371.1--dc23
LC record available at https://lccn.loc.gov/2020007869

ISBN 978-0-8077-6406-0 (paper)
ISBN 978-0-8077-6407-7 (hardcover)
ISBN 978-0-8077-7865-4 (ebook)

Printed on acid-free paper
Manufactured in the United States of America

Becoming a Metacognitive Teacher

To Dave and Liam.

—Roya

To Teachers Everywhere.

—DeVere

To Allison and Anna.

—Seth

Contents

Foreword

Most of us go into teaching because we loved one of our former teachers: She made it look so easy! As a teacher educator, I always had difficulty convincing my teacher candidates that good classroom teachers are not born; they are made, and that, in fact, teaching is hard. From the time when I had my first student teacher as a 6th-grade teacher in 1959, to later when I supervised two student teachers every semester as a lab school teacher, and even later when I taught reading methods, my teacher candidates always seemed to arrive thinking teaching is easy (and you get your summers off). I would have done a much better job of convincing them of the reality of classroom life if my students had had this book. It emphasizes that teaching is a deadly serious, demanding, thoughtful, pragmatic art. It pulls no punches about how difficult it is to create a productive learning environment for the 20–30 divergent students under your care in the harried environment of classrooms, and that to succeed you need a proactive, focused mental stance, a reflective, thoughtful approach, and the energy to orchestrate multiple pedagogical variables in response to constantly varying conditions. All that may sound intimidating, but this book takes you by the hand and leads you through. So yes, my prospective teachers would have been much better prepared with this book. You will be too.

Gerald G. Duffy
Professor Emeritus
Michigan State University

Preface

This user-friendly, research-based guide is intended mainly for candidates in teacher preparation programs. We want to help them navigate coursework, build relationships with mentors, negotiate fieldwork and student teaching, and effectively apply these experiences to their own classroom teaching so they can become metacognitive teachers. Novice teachers may also find this resource useful because they are striving to implement learning from their coursework while becoming familiar with their new teaching contexts. Candidates and novice teachers may welcome guidance from this resource because every aspect of being—or becoming—a teacher can feel new and potentially overwhelming. Candidates could use this as a course text or supplementary text for introductory education courses, as well as in seminars that accompany field experiences. This book could also be a resource that candidates review and then try out concepts as an independent study project that surpasses course requirements. Novices could use this resource as a text that accompanies professional development sessions for new teachers. Candidates and novices could opt to select this resource to learn about metacognitive teaching on their own or as part of a book club choice.

In addition, mentor teachers, cooperating teachers, administrators, and instructional coaches could benefit from this book because they may have forgotten how overwhelming the journey into teaching can be or they may not realize how much teacher preparation programs have changed since they began their own journeys. Mentors, cooperating teachers, administrators, and instructional coaches can use this resource as a book club selection. They can discuss it with one another, such as about how they support—and how they can better support—candidates, student teachers, and novice teachers along their journeys to becoming metacognitive teachers. These leaders could require the resource as a book club for all candidates, student teachers, and novice teachers in their school to stimulate discussion about teaching and learning through the lens of metacognitive teaching.

Teacher educators, too, could use this book to help them focus on being more explicit as to how each component of their teacher preparation builds on the next to promote metacognitive teaching in their courses, as well as across their preparation programs. Teacher educators may form their own book club to discuss across the program faculty the issue of how the program supports candidates' journeys to becoming metacognitive teachers. Examples and resources throughout the chapters could be used by teacher educators in class sessions to promote candidates' thinking about how they are becoming metacognitive teachers. Further, this resource may help teacher educators reflect on their own journeys to becoming metacognitive teachers.

Acknowledgments

We wish to thank the teacher candidates, student teachers, novice teachers, mentor teachers, and university instructor colleagues whose voices are heard throughout this book. We spent years studying the teacher candidates' journeys into their first teaching position, and we are grateful for their willingness to participate in our longitudinal research studies. We used pseudonyms throughout this book to keep the names of individuals and universities confidential. We provided a teacher colleague the pseudonym Danny and a mentor teacher the pseudonym Ms. Jackson. One colleague's real name appears in this book: Janet Young. We mention Ms. Howard, who is a real classroom teacher. Additional teachers' voices appear in this book and, with permission, we used their real names: Tori Golden, Joanna Lin, and Amber Moss. We sometimes refer to ourselves by our first names: Roya, DeVere, and Seth.

We deeply appreciate our colleagues from the Literacy Research Association's Teacher Education Research Study Group (TERSG), as well as colleagues from the Association of Literacy Educators and Researchers who worked alongside us to gather and analyze data. Those colleagues include Sandra A. Chambers, Beth Dobler, Dana L. Grisham, Susan J. Lenski, Jacquelynn Malloy, Melissa Pierczynski, W. David Scales, Linda Smetana, Margaret Vaughn, Karen Kreider Yoder, and Janet R. Young. Their dedication to the realm of literacy education and teacher preparation inspires us and we are honored to call them our colleagues.

We are thankful to Brian Wolsey for turning our rough ink sketches of the metacognitive teaching model into a graphic that captured our thinking perfectly (see Chapter 1). Brian's talent with graphic design is astonishing, and we appreciate his support.

We wish to acknowledge our Teachers College Press editorial team, especially Emily Spangler, Caritza Berlioz, Susan Liddicoat, and Lori Tate, as well as others who worked behind the scenes. We also appreciate the reviewers whose feedback guided our thinking as this book moved from thoughts to reality.

Evidence-Based and Metacognitive Teaching

A Brief Overview

Teaching is more than a career, more than an adventure or journey. From the first day you walk into the classroom until the day you retire, it is an exploration. Every day, every class, and every school year leads to new learning. So, if you want to be a teacher or if you are already teaching, we have some questions for you. First off, *Why teach?* You may have heard that question a thousand times already. Maybe someone has tried to persuade you to do something—anything—besides teaching. But you want to teach because. . . . Take a few minutes to dig deep and truly consider your *why*. Follow the link or QR code in Figure 1.1 to watch the 3-minute Michael Jr. video as you consider your *why*.

As comedian Michael Jr. says, "When you know your *why*, your *what* has more impact because you're walking in or toward your purpose." Your *what* is teaching. The goal you hope to accomplish through teaching, such as changing the world for the better somehow, promoting a love for learning, or saving the whales, is your *why*. Some experts in teacher education (e.g., Duffy, 2005; Malloy, Marinak, & Gambrell, 2019; Parsons, Vaughn, Malloy, & Pierczynski, 2017) call the *why* your *vision* for teaching. Teachers with a vision (their *why*) are able to overcome challenges they face in their career because they are grounded in their purpose and they are passionate about it. If you don't have your *why* firmly in mind yet, continue to consider your purpose for teaching.

CONSIDERING YOUR PLANS FOR TEACHING

What kind of teacher do you want to be? You've probably thought about what grade level you want to teach and your favorite subject matter (science, math, social studies, reading, writing, or others). What else do you need to consider? Hopefully, you're thinking that you want to be a "good" teacher. What does "good" mean to you? Let's use the word *effective* instead

Figure 1.1. Link and QR code for Michael Jr.: Know Your Why

www.youtube.com/watch?v=LZe5y2D60YU

of *good*. What does "effective" teaching look like and sound like? Think about your favorite teacher.

- How did that person inspire you to want to teach?
- Why was that teacher your favorite?
- What did he or she teach you? (think beyond academics)
- What was the teacher's impact on your learning?
- Do you remember that teacher making the job look easy?

Most of the teacher candidates we encounter say that they thought teaching would be easy because their teachers made it seem that way. For example, teacher candidate Wendy shared the following in an interview:

> I came into the program thinking that, I mean I don't want to sound arrogant, but thinking that I already knew a lot of the things that I needed to know. I guess I didn't. You don't always remember exactly how you learned things and how those skills built up as you went because now at this point it's just become such a part of you, so I guess I just kind of took for granted the teaching that went into my learning like all the work that my teachers did.

Recognizing Effective Teachers

Chances are, your favorite teacher—the one who inspired you or changed your life somehow—is probably an effective teacher. *Effective teachers* understand and navigate the classroom complexity well because they are metacognitive. That is, effective teachers reflect on their lessons (while they are teaching and afterward) and can adapt lessons immediately if they can tell that their students need something different. For example, some students might need more examples, more explanations, different materials, or for the lesson to change altogether. What if a teacher starts a lesson and realizes that it's too easy for the students? Does the teacher continue the lesson anyway? Or does the teacher change instruction so the content is something the students need to learn?

Teacher candidate Wendy explained that she didn't realize all the pieces that went into teaching. She wasn't expecting how much was involved. Wendy said:

> I look back and I realize, oh that's what [my own K–12 teachers] were doing, that's why that worked, so there's a lot more to teaching than I expected. It's a harder process than I thought, and there's a lot of planning and a lot of preparation that goes into it. You have to know your students so individually with those needs. I mean there's so many different possibilities and skills that you have to cover. I guess I feel like [because of my program], . . . I'm so much more aware of all the needs that my students are going to have.

Learning to Be an Effective Teacher

We authors have learned from and with teacher candidates across the United States and around the world. We followed them through their education courses, through student teaching, and then into their first years of teaching. We have found that teachers who are technical in their teaching (e.g., following lesson plans without adjustments) do not have their vision for teaching in mind. That is, they don't know *why* they are teaching. They get frustrated because they cannot adjust to the complexity of the teaching context (classroom, school, and district). Sadly, they often leave the profession. We want to help you become an effective teacher.

Teachers often reflect on the preparation programs that led them to their first classroom. Some professors stand out, and cooperating (mentor) teachers leave lasting impressions on the teacher the candidate will become. Thinking about your own experience, take a minute to ponder the following questions:

- Which professors in your teacher preparation program have inspired you? How have they inspired you?
- How have those inspiring professors connected the person you are with the teacher you want to be (or are in process of becoming)?
- Which mentor teachers have shown you a path that you hadn't seen before?

Teacher candidate Carrie shared that she's taking all her learning about teaching to think about her teaching:

> Our program has given me a lot of good ideas, and I think that right now I see myself kind of following a lot of those ideas, but—right now—I don't have a set plan. I don't know. I guess I'm still forming what I want my classroom to look like and a lot of it will have to do with the needs of my students.

This book is a guide to help you on your journey to effective teaching as you fit coursework and field-based experiences together in a meaningful way so that each experience directly leads to professional growth as a metacognitive teacher. What does *metacognitive teaching* mean?

Metacognitive teaching requires higher-level thought processes, in which teachers continuously reflect on and monitor their teaching practices while making changes, or adaptations, to their lessons, based on their students' learning needs. These adaptations happen while teachers are teaching, and they can also happen as the teacher reflects on how the lesson went and thinks about changes to make for the next lesson.

REFLECTING ON TEACHING

So far, we have used the verb *reflect* several times. This is a good place to stop and examine just what we mean by "reflect" and its associated noun "reflection." *Reflection* is a critical component of learning and developing the ability for abstract thought. Reflection differs from situation to situation, and an effective reflection asks the thinker to bring cognitive resources to bear. Romer (2003), describing Schön's (1983) model of professional reflection, proposes that teaching practice is more than learning about educational theories. Indeed, teachers constantly learn from and reflect on their teaching through their situated experiences. Teachers often struggle with many teaching models and paradigms that sometimes conflict with one another as they try to meet the learning needs of their students. Multiple stakeholders, such as parents, school administrators, and policymakers, add to the complexity of teaching.

One way to help bring coherence and unity to the complex act of teaching is through reflection. "The learning process may then be described as a circular structure involving the elements of framing, experiment, situational backtalk, evaluation, and reframing. This process may of course go on infinitely" (Romer, 2003, p. 86).

Teachers often state, quite correctly, that they are always learners. Learning to teach and learning to adjust one's teaching are characteristics that may be informed by a reflective structure. If teachers think about their starting position as a frame of reference, then tinker with the conceptual knowledge, support or push back against the notions they encounter, evaluate the evolving concepts, and reframe their thinking, we can say that learning to be a more informed teacher has occurred. More important, the mental adjustments made through reflective learning are likely to transfer to new conditions and situations.

Reflection and metacognitive teaching complement each other perfectly. *Reflection*, much more than just recalling events, allows teachers to assess how their teaching proceeded, and *metacognition* permits the teacher to look forward and adjust, often right in the heat of the teaching moment. We elaborate on the metacognitive teaching cycle in Chapter 3.

We have studied teacher effectiveness and teacher preparation programs that equip teacher candidates to be inspiring teachers. While our specialty is literacy, the guidance we provide is applicable to teaching in other content areas. Our 3-year longitudinal study involved surveys of 300 teacher candidates, interviews with 15 teacher candidates, interviews with faculty members of teacher preparation programs, interviews and observations of 15 student teachers and seven novice teachers, and interviews with 15 cooperating teachers. We followed seven teacher candidates through their programs and into their novice teaching years. Throughout the study, we found that the most effective new teachers were the ones who could adjust to the ever-changing environment of the classroom. We call this ability to adapt and adjust, tweak and regroup, push and pull at the same time *metacognitive teaching*.

THINKING ABOUT METACOGNITION

Metacognition is commonly defined as thinking about one's own thinking (e.g., Cornish & Jenkins, 2012; Duffy, 2005; Griffith, 2017). As we have explained, metacognitive teaching involves higher-level thought processes, in which teachers continuously reflect on and monitor their instructional practices while flexibly adapting to the complexity of their teaching contexts, especially when attending to students' instructional needs. That is, metacognitive teachers have the "ability to reflect on their teaching (i.e., monitor it) and improve teaching on the basis of reflections" (Pressley, 2005, p. 394). Thus metacognitive teachers are proactive by thoughtfully adapting their instruction in the moment, based on their quick decision-making from their ongoing reflections of students' performance.

Metacognitive Teachers Take Charge

In this era of high-stakes accountability, schools are unfortunately judged based almost entirely on students' test scores. While this is only one small indicator of student performance, teachers' knowledge, skills, and instructional actions are deemed as direct influences on those scores. Frequently, teachers are told to follow curricular "scripts," so they may not even see a benefit in thinking about their teaching. What could be done to rectify that? Teacher candidates ought to be aware of their processes of learning to teach in order to help them become metacognitive teachers, and their voices should be heard and honored. Indeed, Duffy (2005) asserts that "rather than creating passive users of knowledge who apply what they know in procedural ways, metacognition offers the possibility of creating teachers who possess the proactive state of mind and the emotional strength to 'take charge'" (p. 301).

Metacognitive Teachers Adapt

Effective teaching has received much attention, with studies of practicing K–12 classroom teachers finding specific aspects of classroom instruction to be best practices or effective strategies. For instance, Vaughn, Parsons, Gallagher, and Branen (2016) indicate that metacognitive teachers are effective teachers because they adapt their instruction while teaching, where they "quickly reflect, analyze, and determine a student's needs based upon pedagogical expertise and their knowledge of their students" (p. 543). While the focus has been on inservice teachers' knowledge, skills, and practices, we believe it is time to bring you (teacher candidates and novice teachers) into this important conversation and empower you to become metacognitive teachers in your first teaching assignments.

As we have explained, teachers with a vision (their *why*) are able to overcome challenges they face in their career because they are grounded in their purpose and they are passionate about it. Metacognitive teachers have a vision that sustains them in the complexity of teaching. Teachers without a vision often leave the profession because they cannot adjust to the complexity of teaching. This is evident in teacher turnover rates. These rates are alarming, with beginning teacher attrition higher than teachers with experience. For instance, the attrition rate for beginning teachers across North Carolina is 12.34%, which is 59% higher than experienced teachers' attrition rates (Henkel, 2019). *A Coming Crisis in Teaching?* (Sutcher, Darling-Hammond, & Carver-Thomas, 2016) reports that some states (e.g., Arizona, Utah) already have a teacher shortage crisis, and the authors predict this will become worse over time, nationwide.

Factors Leading to Metacognitive Teaching

In this book our overarching goal is to provide research-based evidence of key contributing factors that lead to metacognitive teaching as you, as a future teacher, journey through the teacher candidate to novice teacher stages. For instance, in our longitudinal research described earlier, we discovered that some candidates had the mindset of program "completion" and became technical in their teaching, whereas others made the most of trying to fit all the pieces together. The latter became truly metacognitive teachers.

As we began writing this book, we noted that there are many books that talk about "surviving" the first years of teaching. We think that new teachers need to do more than just survive. They should thrive in their classrooms, make professional decisions that no script will ever replicate, and become champions for their students. If that description matches your vision of teaching, then this book can be your guide as you navigate coursework,

Figure 1.2. The Metacognitive Teaching Journey

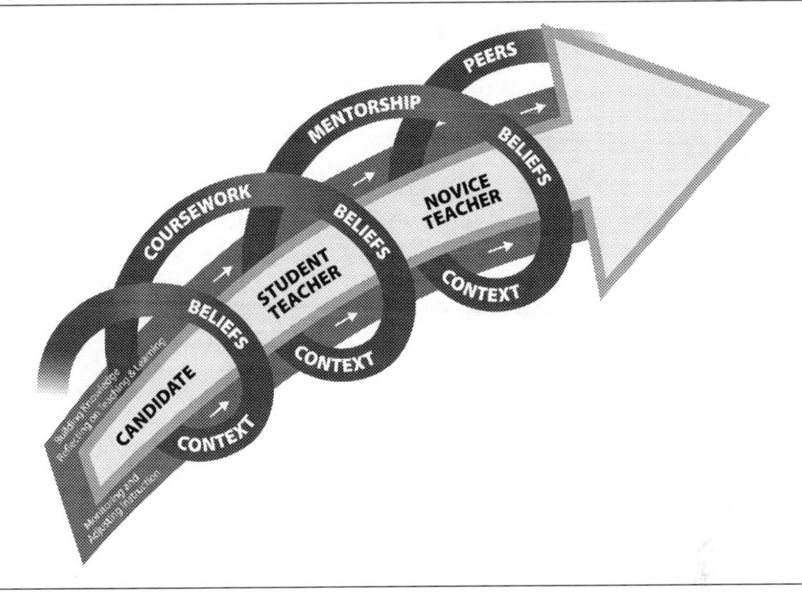

Note. Adapted from "Are we preparing or training teachers?: Developing professional judgment in and beyond teacher preparation programs," by R. Q. Scales, T. D.,Wolsey, S. Lenski, L. Smetana, K. K. Yoder, E. Dobler, . . . J. Young, 2018,. *Journal of Teacher Education*, *69*(1), 7–21. doi:10.1177/0022487117702584

build relationships with mentors, negotiate fieldwork and student teaching, and make connections between these experiences as you become metacognitive novice teachers.

Figure 1.2 represents our view of the teacher's journey into teaching. Perhaps the first thing you will notice in the figure is the path from teacher candidate to student teacher to novice teacher and beyond. Next, you'll wonder why "context" appears below each of the stages of the teaching journey. In our own teaching and in our work with teachers, we noticed that whom you teach and where you teach have a tremendous impact on teacher effectiveness. That is, the school, classroom, and students are important parts of the context, along with your teacher preparation program.

Continuing to follow the trajectory in Figure 1.2, your "beliefs" are ever-present throughout your journey into teaching. Those beliefs are shaped by your coursework, your peers (classmates, mentor teachers, colleagues), and your context.

In Figure 1.2 the goal of metacognitive teaching encloses the progression through the teaching stages. You can begin by being intentional in reflecting on your "building knowledge," while "monitoring and adjusting your instruction," as you enter the classroom. Figure 1.2 illustrates your teaching journey with an arrow pointing into the future because the trajectory is ongoing. Metacognitive teaching is not an end goal that you eventually reach. Instead, metacognitive teaching requires the components included in Figure 1.2.

Follow the Evidence

"I'll know more when I get him to autopsy," the medical examiner in almost every crime-procedural program on television says when a body is discovered and the initial evidence is not sufficient. Like the coroner in these series, teachers should also follow the evidence. Fortunately, the evidence doesn't involve an autopsy table if you're a teacher candidate or teacher. And, there is plenty of evidence on which you can rely as you make professional decisions, such as the following:

- Your coursework during the teacher preparation program is an excellent foundational source of useful information. In Chapter 3 we will explore how to make the most of a program.
- Articles in professional journals that are reviewed by professors and teachers in the field are another excellent source of evidence to support the decisions you make. From these, you will learn the broad strokes of teaching and specific ideas you can use or adapt to your own teaching situation.
- Professional associations provide a wealth of opportunities to continue your learning about teaching. Besides reading their journals, you can attend their annual conferences to connect with other teachers as you seek professional development. We encourage you to join one or more that fits your teaching needs. A list of some of these organizations can be found in Figure 1.3. If you are in a teacher preparation program, you might qualify for a student discount on the membership fee, so be sure to ask about it.
- When you are in the classroom, the work your students do and your observations of that work can inform your decision process. In Chapter 6 we will explore what to observe and how to make good use of what you see and your students do.
- As a novice teacher, seek out other teachers in your school and district who know the ropes specific to your school. If you have an assigned mentor, stay in close touch. If not, buddy up with a teacher whose experience you trust.

Throughout this book, we plan to explore with you several aspects of becoming a teacher. Evidence from our longitudinal research shows that some candidates and teachers found it easier to become metacognitive about their teaching, while other candidates and teachers were more technical. As explained in the next section, we aim to provide you with a roadmap

Figure 1.3. List of Professional Associations in Education

Name	Website URL	QR code
American Council on the Teaching of Foreign Languages (ACTFL)	www.actfl.org	
Additional associations for specific languages—Link page	www.scolt.org/scolt-state-organizations	
American Educational Research Association (AERA)	www.aera.net/	
American Federation of Teachers (AFT)	www.aft.org	
American Library Association (ALA)	www.ala.org/	
Association for Learning Environments (A4LE)	www.a4le.org//	
Association for Middle Level Education (AMLE)	www.amle.org/	

Association for Supervision and Curriculum Development (ASCD)	www.ascd.org	
Association of Literacy Educators and Researchers (ALER)	www.aleronline.org	
California Reading Association (CRA)	californiareading.org	
International Literacy Association (ILA)	www.literacyworld-wide.org/	
International Society for Technology in Education (ISTE)	www.iste.org	
Literacy Research Association (LRA)	www.literacyresear-chassociation.org	
National Association for the Education of Young Children (NAEYC)	www.naeyc.org/	

National Association of Special Education Teachers (NASET)	www.naset.org	
National Council of Teachers of English (NCTE)	www.ncte.org	
National Council of Teachers of Mathematics (NCTM)	www.nctm.org	
National Education Association (NEA)	www.nea.org	
National Science Teaching Association (NSTA)	www.nsta.org/	
National Council for the Social Studies (NCSS)	www.socialstudies.org	
Society of Health and Physical Educators (SHAPE America); Formerly the American Alliance for Health, Physical Education, Recreation, and Dance	www.shapeamerica.org	

TESOL International Association (TESOL); formerly Teachers of English to Speakers of Other Languages	www.tesol.org	

toward developing the professional judgment you need to become a truly metacognitive teacher.

HOW TO MAKE THE MOST OF THIS BOOK

In this book we investigate how your teacher preparation coursework, your teaching mentors (we bet there are many!), and your peers and school colleagues affect how well you do your work as a teacher. We encourage you to look ahead to see what the next part of your journey entails and to reread sections for new insights and to reflect on your growth and development as a metacognitive teacher.

Each chapter includes vignettes and extended interview comments from teacher candidates, student teachers, novice teachers, and mentor teachers that demonstrate metacognitive teaching. Reading about the experiences of those who have made this journey before you will build your confidence. All chapters present evidence-based content with findings tailored to the teacher candidate journey and what the implications are for teacher candidates in becoming metacognitive teachers. As useful as examples and anecdotes are, what research tells us about good teaching should be foundational to your teaching development. Reflection opportunities throughout this book promote direct connections to your own teaching and learning contexts, with the purpose of discovering how you are becoming a metacognitive teacher.

Knowing how the chapters are formatted can help you attend to the most important sections for you. Each chapter has the following special features:

- *Anticipating the Chapter Topics.* At the beginning of the chapter this list of questions provides an indication of the content to come.
- *Reflecting on This Chapter.* At the end of the chapter text, reflection questions promote metacognitive thinking about your teaching.
- *Further Readings and Resources.* At the end of the chapter, lists of printed and electronic sources enable you to continue to explore your special interests in teaching.

Chapter Overviews

An overview of each of the following chapters appears below. Knowing what is coming up next can help you plan how to navigate this book and perhaps the chapters of your teaching career.

Chapter 2: How teacher candidates can develop metacognitive teaching practices as they progress from student teaching to novice teaching.
Chapter 3: How teacher candidates can navigate coursework and the implications for their development as metacognitive teachers.
Chapter 4: How teacher candidates and student teachers can navigate the complexity of still being a student while moving into the role of teacher.
Chapter 5: How teacher candidates can adapt their learning from coursework to meet students' learning needs while reflecting on their practices.
Chapter 6: How student teachers and novice teachers can flexibly use professional judgment to meet students' learning needs (e.g., differentiating instruction, making adaptations in the moment) and how as metacognitive teachers they handle the complexity of changing teaching contexts.
Chapter 7: How you can learn from teacher candidates' journeys in becoming metacognitive teachers and what that means for your own teaching journey.

Additional Resources

At the end of the text we have provided additional resources. The Appendix provides lists of supplementary materials for course instructors, mentor teachers, instructional coaches, and administrators. These materials are organized by chapter and mainly include journal articles, blogs, and videos. We also encourage teacher candidates, student teachers, and novice teachers to explore these resources.

We want to draw your attention to the Glossary that will help you learn the terms that are specific to teaching and learning. Keep in mind that some concepts that represent approximately the same information may use different terms depending on your school setting and teacher preparation program.

Quite often, readers who get to the end of a book just skip over the References, or bibliography. We challenge you to make use of the reference list. Ask yourself what authors and concepts come up often as you read this book and others in your professional library. Become familiar with the seminal pieces and which journals or publishers put them into print.

An index, of course, is a great tool for finding the exact part of the book you need to refresh your memory or consult for further insight. Finally, be sure to read about us and learn how to contact us with your thoughts and suggestions in About the Authors.

CONTEMPLATE THIS VISION OF TEACHING

To provide a closing to this introductory chapter, we asked Johann Henry, a middle school teacher, to share his thoughts on what makes teachers effective. After reading what he told us below, think about the teachers and professors who inspired you: Which aspects of teaching does Johann connect with your vision of teaching?

> To become a teacher, means to no longer think of yourself first. You now belong to the community of people who actively *invest* in the spiritual, academic, and physical well-being of others. When I speak of the spiritual aspect, I am referring to the intentions of your heart. Students can tell when they are working with someone who really cares about building their character and academic advancements as opposed to doing the bare minimum to receive their paycheck.
>
> One of the most important things a teacher can do is *trust* that the students are listening to the instruction. Use all the advanced academic language and higher-level thinking as possible so that the students can rise to the level they need to be. We as teachers have to believe and act upon the knowledge that every student has the ability to learn the content with all its subtle nuances. Even when the students are not getting the ideas and keep making mistakes, here lies the excitement of creating informal assessments and exercises with your colleagues to help the students achieve the learning goals.
>
> Finally, new and veteran teachers must be excited about *learning* from their students and colleagues. Allowing students to witness your growth as a teacher by first recognizing whatever positive contribution they make to the culture of the classroom is critical for instruction. Talking politely to a misbehaving student, putting effort in answering a question, acknowledging a talkative student finally getting work done quietly—such actions will boost the morale of the class and encourage the students to be willing participants in the classroom learning environment.

FURTHER READINGS AND RESOURCES

Articles

Duffy, G. G. (1998). Teaching and the balancing of round stones. *Phi Delta Kappan*, *79*(10), 777–780. Retrieved from eric.ed.gov/?id=EJ566244

Read this journal article to learn more about teacher visioning and why it's important for teachers to have a vision for teaching. As you read, consider your own vision and how you will use it as a touchstone when the school year gets complicated.

Griffith, R., & Lacina, J. (2017). Teacher as decision maker: A framework to guide teaching decisions in reading. *The Reading Teacher*, *71*(4), 501–507. doi.org/10.1002/trtr.1662

As you read this article, consider the model the authors present and how it translates into content areas beyond reading. Think about how you can use the framework presented to inform your teaching decisions.

Blogs

Mulvahill, E. (2019, July 3). How a vision board can help guide you through teaching's ups and downs: A visual representation of your dreams, values, and aspirations.

Read this blog post and consider making your own vision board to use as a physical representation of your vision—your ultimate purpose for teaching.

www.weareteachers.com/teacher-vision-board/

TED Playlists. (n.d.). TED Talks Education.

TED Talks Education is a playlist of several videos specifically related to teaching.We highly recommend that you begin with watching Rita Pierson's TED Talk "Every kid needs a champion" and consider your vision (your "why" or purpose for teaching) as you watch this video. Videos range from 6–19 minutes.

www.ted.com/playlists/125/tv_special_ted_talks_educatio

CHAPTER 2

Metacognitive Practice from Student Teaching to Novice Teaching

Fitting the Pieces Together

Anticipating the Chapter Topics

- What is metacognitive teaching, and why is it important?
- What knowledge and dispositions do metacognitive teachers have?

YOUR TRANSITIONING ROLE

During your teacher preparation coursework, you are a student who is thinking about many things. You have to complete prerequisite courses; you have to complete methods courses; you have to arrange practicum experiences; you have additional coursework; you have familial and social activities; you may have a job; and more. When you move into student teaching, everything escalates. In addition to being a student, you are expected to also transition into the role of a teacher. Suddenly you are in someone else's classroom; the school has specific initiatives and approaches; you likely have specific instructional practices that you have to complete for the college or university; you have to attend staff meetings, grade-level meetings, IEP meetings, parent meetings, back-to-school nights, and more. You may still have college courses to complete, a job, familial responsibilities, civic duties, philanthropic work, and so on. When you move into your first year of teaching, demands escalate even more. You will likely move to a new school that has new initiatives and approaches; you no longer have the scaffolds of your university supervisor and mentor (cooperating) teacher; you have full and total responsibility for all instructional duties; you have new students; and so on. We recognize that many transitions take place in a short amount of time (from being admitted to your program to starting your first year of teaching) and this can seem overwhelming.

Thinking in the Classroom

Over the next several years, you have a lot on your plate and a lot on your mind. What this book focuses on, though, is your thinking in the classroom. You've spent a lot of time in classrooms. Take a minute to think about a specific incident from elementary school. What were you doing? What were your peers doing? What were you supposed to be doing? What was the teacher doing? Now think about middle school. Now high school.

As a teacher, you will be crafting and managing these types of situations. You have 20 to 35 students, all of whom have different background knowledge, prior experiences, levels of English proficiency, interests, motivations, and home lives. It is your job to design and implement instruction that meets all students' learning needs to move them toward proficiency on state standards. This is a nuanced and complex task. We know from theory and our previous research the types of instruction that support learning and motivation: teaching that includes explicit explanations of skills, strategies, and content embedded in authentic learning situations. By explicit explanations, we mean that you should reveal your own thought processes as you reveal how the skills, strategies, and content work. This careful modeling followed by scaffolding (structured assistance where students practice with you) promotes students' learning because you demystify the processes involved (Duffy, 2014). Scaffolding is structured assistance to build students' success during lessons. That follows modeling because scaffolding provides opportunities where students practice the concept with your careful guidance and input, which means their understandings of the concepts are reinforced. Lessons should include modeling and scaffolding, with ample opportunities for discovery, discussion, choice, collaboration, and feedback. For authentic learning situations, strive to create lessons that provide experiences that closely replicate how students would apply their learning outside of school settings. Once students realize that lessons in school directly connect to their navigation of the world beyond your classroom walls, and especially to what interests them, they tend to see the value in education and want to learn more (Guthrie & Barber, 2019).

Developing Metacognitive Awareness

You will learn about principles of effective instruction in your teacher preparation coursework, in your textbooks, and in other professional books. This book supports you as you develop the metacognitive awareness that allows you to effectively navigate instruction. Consider the following example from Isabel, a student teacher at the end of her student teaching experience in a 1st-grade classroom. She and her mentor teacher have designed an animal project that integrates science and literacy. They spent several class sessions "previewing" different animals and teaching students the different characteristics of animals (type of skin/fur, diet, shelter, group interactions, and so on). Over the next week, students then did research to create an *All About . . .* book of their chosen animal. Let's take a peek into one of those classes when students are working on their animal books:

> The classroom is lively with chatter as students work in table groups. This lesson is during Isabel's formal student teaching, so she is the only teacher in the classroom. The table groups have access to different materials based upon where they are in creating their book. One group has laptop computers that students are using to search *Britannica Kids* for information about their animal. One group has paper, scissors, crayons, tape, and glue; they are beginning to illustrate their books and put the books together. Another group is writing the text for their books, which they will complete before adding illustrations.
>
> Isabel circulates around the classroom, observing student behavior and assessing their understanding and progress. She asks questions, provides modeling, gives direct instruction, and provides specific feedback on students' progress. Isabel notices that several students across all three groups are lacking detail in their notes or writing. She decides to pull these students for a small-group lesson on adding detail. Isabel is quickly thinking about a text she could use as a model as she calls them over to the table. Just as she's doing this, Franco, who is in the illustrating group, tells Isabel that he is tired of alligators and wants to change animals. She must consider where they are in this unit (i.e., how many more days does Franco have if he starts from the beginning), what she knows about Franco, the purposes of the unit, motivational considerations, whether this will lead to other students wanting to change animals, and so on—all in a matter of seconds as she pulls the "detail" group and picks a model text.

Reread the second half of the teaching example, starting at "Isabel circulates around the classroom. . . ." This is an example of teaching metacognitively. Isabel was monitoring students and assessing their understanding and making small adjustments (e.g., giving feedback) and more substantive adjustments or additions (e.g., pulling a small group) to her instruction accordingly. She was also considering and addressing unanticipated student questions, such as Franco's request to change animals. As Isabel's teaching example shows, teaching is no easy task. It is multifaceted and unpredictable, which is why it is necessary for teachers to be metacognitive to effectively meet students' learning needs.

METACOGNITION AND METACOGNITIVE TEACHING

As defined in Chapter 1, *metacognition* is thinking about one's own thinking. Applied to teachers, it is the thinking teachers do in the classroom, using the knowledge they have of the curriculum, content, pedagogy, and their students to make numerous instructional decisions, both large and small, minute by minute and day by day—just as Isabel was doing in the teaching example above. Teacher metacognition is a skill that develops over time. It is quite difficult to teach metacognitively early in your program. Although you are completing field experiences and teaching lessons in those experiences, early in your program you are mainly observing and teaching only periodically in different grade levels. Those experiences are important and necessary because they help you better understand the work of teaching. Observing and teaching just a few lessons, however, precludes the deep knowledge of teaching, students, and curriculum that is necessary to be intentional and effective in adjusting your instruction on the fly, as exhibited by Isabel. Once you get to student teaching, you will likely spend several weeks or months in a classroom before taking over full instructional responsibility. By that time in your teacher education program, you will have methods coursework behind you, and you will implement your learning from those courses in your student teaching. Being fully part of a classroom every day will provide you with the practical knowledge of teaching, curriculum, and students, which means you will have the opportunity to teach metacognitively.

TEACHER KNOWLEDGE AND METACOGNITIVE TEACHING

As you have likely noticed, metacognitive teaching requires strong knowledge in different areas. It requires strong pedagogical knowledge. *Pedagogy* is the science of teaching, or the instructional methods used to teach. It's not enough to simply know content. You also need to know *how* to teach that content. For example, you might excel in math but that doesn't mean that you know how to teach math. In your education coursework you are learning pedagogy so you will know how to teach. Teacher preparation programs tend to provide separate methods courses for the different content areas (e.g., art methods, language arts methods, math methods, music methods, physical education methods, reading methods, science methods, social studies methods) because the pedagogy (how to teach) differs by subject. While there is no one right way to teach in any content area, your methods coursework will expose you to a variety of approaches to teaching. As the teacher, you will choose the methods for teaching your students based on their learning needs. Consider the different teaching methods (pedagogy) you would need to know for teaching the following lessons:

- *Art:* Teaching students how to critique and refine works of art
- *Language Arts:* Teaching students how to choose a topic for writing a poem
- *Math:* Teaching students how to determine what size rug will fit in the room based on calculating the area
- *Music:* Teaching students how to create rhythmic compositions
- *Physical Education:* Teaching students how to dribble a soccer ball
- *Reading:* Teaching students how to improve their oral reading fluency
- *Science:* Teaching students how to analyze data from their experiments to support or refute ideas
- *Social Studies:* Teaching students how to explain changes over time through analysis of historical narratives

What do you hope to teach? *How* will you teach? Methods courses may require you to develop lesson plans where you demonstrate that you understand how to teach that content area. You may also have opportunities to teach those lessons in a field placement, depending on your program requirements. As you gain experience with developing lesson plans and teaching those plans, you will become more confident with *how* to teach.

Pedagogy is the knowledge of different types of instructional practices (teaching methods) that are effective with different types of learners. As a teacher, you must find out what your students already understand and what they need to learn so you know what to teach. That means you need to understand how to use assessments to shape what and how you teach. Your students will have different learning needs, regardless of grade level and content area(s). Knowledge of pedagogy requires knowledge of assessment because that is vital to designing lessons using appropriate teaching methods that meet students' diverse needs.

In one of our interviews with novice teachers, Rachel explained how she used assessment data to determine how she would teach her students.

> I think something I've been really successful at is taking a lot of different assessments, a lot of different things I've learned from different places and then utilizing those to make decisions about my practice. Then using what we have, because we have so many programs here, we have a closet just stuffed full of stuff and picking what I think will help the individual students best. Because I work in such small groups that I have the ability to do that . . . targeting [resources] to what they need.

Rachel learned about a variety of assessments from methods coursework, from mentor teachers during field placements and student teaching, and from the school where she was hired to teach. From those experiences, Rachel understood how to make decisions about which assessments to use with her students and why they were important. You may be hired into a situation like Rachel's where you have the flexibility to choose from a variety of assessments, or you may be presented with a set of required assessments. Rachel thoughtfully tailored her instruction (teaching methods) to benefit students. She made the decision that teaching small groups of students would better help their learning because she knew how to group students, based on assessment data.

As a novice teacher, you will rely on your knowledge of pedagogy from your methods coursework, field placements, and student teaching. Know that you will never stop learning how to teach because it is a career-long endeavor. In addition to pedagogy, however, you will need to know the curriculum and your students.

Knowledge of Curriculum

Metacognitive teaching also requires strong knowledge of curriculum. The curriculum is guided by state standards as to subject matter that teachers are expected to cover. The standards vary by state and by grade level. States, districts, and schools often provide resources to support teachers in learning and covering standards, including pacing guides and instructional materials. When you know what grade level you are going to complete during internships and student teaching, it is important that you carefully review the standards and any resources provided. It is also often helpful to review the standards of the grades above and below your grade level. This will allow you to know what students are supposed to have learned and where they are heading.

Knowledge of Students

Finally, metacognitive teaching requires knowledge of your students. This knowledge is absolutely vital to successfully using metacognitive practices. It is important that you have a strong understanding of child and youth development, so you know what is developmentally appropriate for the age learner you teach. However, you also need to know your students personally. By spending time with students in your classroom every day, you will inevitably get to know your students. You will see their personalities and dispositions; you will learn their interests and motivations; you will see the work they produce; you will learn their strengths and weaknesses; you will see the results of numerous assessments. All these different pieces of "data" will help you make instructional decisions—not just the content and knowledge they may need more exposure to or direct instruction in, but also how to best reach and apply the content. Some students need to be pushed a little bit, but some students will shut down if they are pushed at all. Some students need structures to help them monitor their progress while others do not need such structures because they may feel limited by this or lose their desire to soar. Knowing your students deeply, through daily interactions and through ongoing formative assessment, will allow you to make differentiated instructional decisions that are appropriate for the students you teach.

Because of the importance of knowing your students, we recommend that you are intentional about gathering lots of information about your students and all aspects of their lives. Getting to know your students helps you build connections with them while demonstrating that you care about who they are beyond the classroom walls. Try to answer questions like the ones in the following list, which you may use as a guide for the kind of information you can collect about your students to get to know who they are as people.

- What are their interests outside of school?
- What hobbies do they have?
- What are they passionate about?
- Do they have siblings?
- What are their hopes and dreams?
- What are their fears?
- What are their favorite sports?
- What are their favorite books?
- What are their favorite movies?

To best meet students' learning needs, you need to know the whole child and not just their performance on academic tasks and assessments. See the list below for ideas on how to get to know your students deeply:

- Communicate with their parents or guardians.
- Conduct home visits.
- Create a student questionnaire that they complete.
- Become pen pals with your students.
- Create opportunities in class when students get to share about their out-of-school interests, and listen closely to what they have to say.
- Give lots of opportunities for choices in their learning (i.e., topics for projects, books, group or partner work) and pay attention to their choices.

What are other ways that you can get to know your students as people?

Figure 2.1. Three Ways to Think of Assessment

Type	Clarification
Assessment *of* learning	What did students actually learn as a result of instruction?
Assessment *for* learning	How can I provide assessment that guides students while they learn?
Assessment *as* learning	How can I help students to assess their own learning and reflect on their progress, achievements, and challenge areas?

Note. Assessment *of*, *for*, and *as* learning were first coined by Stiggins. See Stiggins, R. (2005). *Student-involved assessment for learning* (4th ed.). Upper Saddle River, NJ: Pearson.

WHAT ARE THE CHARACTERISTICS OF METACOGNITIVE TEACHERS?

In addition to deep knowledge of pedagogy, curriculum, and students, metacognitive teachers possess other characteristics as well, some of which you may have surmised from the discussion above, but we want to describe them in more detail below.

Assess Consistently

Metacognitive teachers *consistently assess* students' progress in a variety of ways: formative, summative, informal, kid-watching, and so on. You will learn about assessments, including specific types of assessments and their purposes, throughout your methods coursework. High-stakes summative assessments tend to change every 5–10 years, or as the state standards change. Your school will keep you updated on those changes. Assessing students in a variety of ways helps teachers build their knowledge of students' learning and apply effective pedagogy to teach or reteach curricular standards. See Figure 2.1 for three ways to think broadly about assessment. According to O'Connor (2018), there are four main purposes for assessment. We have adapted the list slightly, as follows:

- *Instructional uses*—To clarify learning goals, indicate students' strengths and weaknesses, inform about students' personal-social development, and contribute to student motivation
- *Communicative uses*—To inform parents/guardians about the learning program of the school and how well their children are achieving the intended learning goals
- *Administrative uses*—To determine promotion or graduation, award honors or penalties, establish athletic or other competitive eligibility, and report to other schools, employers, and universities

- *Guidance uses*—To help students make their educational and vocational plans realistically (p. 18)

Reflect

Metacognitive teachers are also *reflective*. Educators have noted that reflection and metacognition are overlapping constructs because they share many features and are symbiotic (Risko, Roskos, & Vukelich, 2005). Reflecting on your teaching means that you are critically thinking back on your instruction and considering what was effective, what was not, how the lesson could have been improved, and what you will do next, in light of this thinking. Our stance is that reflection on teaching can facilitate your metacognitive teaching.

There are many ways to reflect. We know teachers who reflect best through discussion; they like to reflect with a trusted colleague and brainstorm ideas collaboratively. We know teachers who reflect through journal writing; writing down thoughts helps some teachers to process their ideas and brainstorm next steps. We know a teacher with a long commute who uses the voice recorder feature of her phone to record her reflections as she is driving. There is no one best way to reflect. Instead, the important thing is that you are reflecting every day. Regardless of where you are in your journey, try different ways of reflecting (discussion, writing, voice recordings), and figure out what works best for you.

Become Lifelong Learners

Metacognitive teachers are *open to new ideas* and are *lifelong learners*. Classrooms are far different today than when we authors began teaching. Unlike in the past, when teachers essentially closed their doors and did their best, teachers currently have many opportunities for collaboration, professional development, and resources. Student teacher Carrie, who shared her reflections on her preparation program as a teacher candidate in Chapter 1, spoke to us in a subsequent interview about learning new ideas from her cooperating teacher:

> My cooperating teacher's classroom is very much in line with what I've been taught. My teacher is very aware of the research out there. She knows what the children need and she tries to come up with new ways of teaching. She's been teaching for a really long time, and it's amazing to me to see that she still tries to change some of her lessons or some of the things that she teaches because of the research that she's found.

Engage in Continuous Professional Learning

Carrie participated in grade-level team meetings with her cooperating teacher, and she noticed how the team worked together. They talked about teaching strategies that could help students learn, and they reviewed which standards they needed to focus on in the next week.

Teachers who generously host teacher candidates for internships (interns) and student teachers are not just nurturing the next generation of teachers. Those mentor teachers are also continuing their own professional development by learning about methods coursework requirements, planning with their interns and student teachers, observing lessons, and providing feedback. It's a symbiotic relationship because the mentor teachers learn from the interns and student teachers while the interns and student teachers learn from the mentor teachers. Everyone has opportunities to learn from one another when collaborative structures are in place, whether informal or formal. Informal structures could be setting a regular time to talk about teaching and learning with your mentor or teacher colleagues. Some formal structures, described below, include professional learning communities, instructional coaching, and professional organizations.

Professional Learning Communities. Formal structures are professional learning communities or collaborative learning teams where teachers work together to reflect on their instruction and to plan future instruction. One example of this is when all 3rd-grade teachers from across an entire district meet once monthly to discuss standards. Another example is teachers in the same school meeting with their grade-level colleagues. These activities are typically guided by ongoing assessment information and state standards. If you are in a field placement, ask your mentor teacher if you could join the next grade-level team meeting, as Carrie did, or some other professional learning community meeting.

Instructional Coaching. The number of instructional coaches in schools is increasing. Instructional coaches are teacher leaders who have a wealth of knowledge and designated time to support teachers. Seeking help from the instructional coach is a sign of thoughtful, dedicated teachers who want to make sure they are doing everything possible to benefit their students' learning. You will never know everything there is to know about teaching, so embrace the role of lifelong learner and seek ways to hone your instructional practices throughout your career.

Professional Organizations. Professional organizations are another type of support that provides up-to-date information and resources for its members. In Figure 1.3 (Chapter 1) we listed many professional organizations for you to explore. Ask your mentor teachers, colleagues, and professors which professional organizations they recommend. Do some research to see which seem best for you and join a couple. Some organizations are discipline specific, such as the International Literacy Association and the National Council of Teachers of Mathematics. Other organizations are open to any content area, such as the National Association for the Education of Young Children and Association for Supervision and Curriculum Development. There are also state and local organizations that provide more localized supports. Most organizations will have reduced rates for students, so we urge you to join now.

In sum, teachers have multiple supports that they can use to build their knowledge and enhance their instruction, but staying open to new ideas and being a lifelong learner are prerequisites for learning from these supports.

THE EFFECTIVENESS OF METACOGNITIVE TEACHING

There is no denying that teaching is a complex profession. You are working with numerous students with diverse backgrounds who need to meet rigorous standards. Teachers who thrive in the profession are metacognitive teachers. Metacognitive teachers adeptly navigate the complex and unpredictable nature of classroom teaching by using deep knowledge of pedagogy, curriculum, and students. They grow in their knowledge through ongoing student assessment, constant reflection, and a disposition of lifelong learning. Developing this knowledge and these dispositions starting now and throughout your teaching career will support you in becoming a highly effective metacognitive teacher.

Reflecting on This Chapter

- Have you witnessed or experienced metacognitive teaching in your teacher preparation experiences thus far?
    - What did it look like?
    - What are your thoughts about this important aspect of teaching?
- How do you assess your current knowledge of pedagogy, curriculum, and students?
    - How could you strengthen that knowledge?
- How can you add more reflection to your ongoing development?
- Are you open to new ideas?
    - Are you a lifelong learner?
    - What can you do to improve in these dispositions?
- What professional organization(s) do you think you might benefit from joining?

FURTHER READINGS AND RESOURCES

Books

Burns, W. (2017). Classroom community builders: Activities for the first day & beyond. Branford, CT: Alphabet.

Read this book for ideas about getting to know your students, team-building exercises, and tips for creating a positive classroom community.

Wolsey, T. D., Lenski, S., & Grisham, D. L. (2020). Assessment Literacy: An Educator's Guide to Understanding Assessment, K–12. New York, NY: Guilford Press. Available at www.guilford.com/books/Assessment-Literacy/Wolsey-Lenski-Grisham/9781462542079

This clear, no-nonsense book guides current and future teachers through the concepts, tools, methods, and goals of classroom literacy assessment. The expert authors examine the roles of formative, summative, and benchmark assessments; demystify state and national tests and standards; and show how assessment can seamlessly inform instruction.

Wood, C. (2018). *Yardsticks: Child and adolescent development ages 4–14* (4th ed.). Turners Falls, MA: Center for Responsive Schools.

Read this book for a better understanding of child development in neurotypically developing students. In addition to descriptions of traits by age groups, this book also shares suggestions for thematic units than span content areas.

Article

Provini, C. (2012), Best practices for professional learning communities. *Education World*. Available at www.educationworld.com/a_admin/best-practices-for-professional-learning-communities.shtml

Read this brief article to learn more about how effective professional learning communities are structured. Consider how this compares to your experiences and how you can share and talk about this article with your colleagues.

Blogs

H. L. [Screen name]. (2019, January 18). The importance of professional learning communities & how to make them effective.

An assistant principal shared tips for making professional learning communities more effective. Talk about this with your mentor teacher and colleagues so you can decide how to move forward with creating or revising your professional learning community work:

www.schoology.com/blog/importance-professional-learning-communities-how-make-them-effective

Howton, R. (2019, September 1). My three steps for building trust with students.

This blog post features advice from a veteran teacher with 28 years of experience. Think about how you could incorporate some of these tips into your day to get to know your students better.

www.teacher2teacher.education/2019/09/01/my-three-steps-for-building-trust-with-students/

Provenzano, N. (2014, September 25). The reflective teacher: Taking a long look.

Read this post and consider how you learn by reflecting on your teaching and on students' learning. Think about which reflection method you prefer and try it out.

www.edutopia.org/blog/reflective-teacher-taking-long-look-nicholas-provenzano

Woodard, C. (2019, August 7). 6 Strategies for building better student relationships.

Read this post and consider how you can incorporate similar strategies for getting to know students in your classroom.

www.edutopia.org/article/6-strategies-building-better-student-relationships

Videos

Edutopia. (2015, August 25). *Teacher collaboration: Spreading best practices school-wide.*

Watch this short video to see how two elementary teachers collaborated in their planning to benefit students' learning. How can you help build a collaborative relationship with teachers in your school?

www.youtube.com/watch?v=85HUMHBXJf4

Edutopia. (2016, April 20). *Collaborative planning: Integrating curriculum across subjects.*

This video demonstrates how teachers from grades 6–8 work together to integrate subject areas so students can see the relevance of learning throughout the school day. How do you exchange ideas with other teachers to promote deeper learning experiences for students?

www.youtube.com/watch?v=yCy4PSOvkL4

LSU Center for Academic Success. (2013, March 26). *Think about thinking—It's metacognition!*

While this video focuses on metacognition and studying habits rather than teaching, watch it and think about how this applies to you and your learning about teaching.

www.youtube.com/watch?v=P_b44JaBQ-Q

TEDx. (2015, April 9). *Improve learning by thinking about learning | Todd Zakrajsek | TEDxUNC.*

This Tedx Talk provides information about how we learn and how we can improve learning. One thing the speaker repeats is how to train your brain so you are thinking about your thinking. Watch this video and consider how this relates to becoming metacognitive about learning to teach. Specifically, how are you learning about teaching?

www.youtube.com/watch?v=tYg3sLcyLB8

Focusing on Coursework for Professional Background Knowledge

ANTICIPATING THE CHAPTER TOPICS

- What signature aspects of your teacher preparation program align with your values and goals as a teacher-to-be?
- How will you approach and navigate your teaching context?
- What does metacognitive teaching mean for you?

SIGNATURE ASPECTS OF TEACHER PREPARATION PROGRAMS

Why did you choose the teacher preparation program you did? At first, that may seem obvious. Perhaps you live near the university, so the program is convenient to work and home. Maybe your parents or siblings attended the university. Possibly one of your teachers in school talked about the college she attended, and you thought it would be a good program for you, too. We think there may be more factors to consider, though all these reasons and others are important.

A part of our inquiry as researchers into teacher education and preparation programs led us to identify what each program emphasized and why it emphasized those aspects over others (Lenski et al., 2013). We call those areas of emphasis "signature aspects." While each program prepared teacher candidates for work in the classroom, there were significant differences as to what each program thought was important in terms of content and approach. For example, Balfour University faculty in literacy believed that differentiated instruction, reading and writing processes, skilled literacy strategy instruction, and motivation to read should be significant aspects of their teacher preparation program. The teacher preparation program at Balfour also reflected the overall mission of the university to educate for social justice and equity based on standards.

On the other hand, the signature aspects of the teacher preparation program in literacy at Montbalm University included teaching candidates how to translate theory into practice, teach using balanced literacy approaches, assess student progress to inform instruction, and build learning communities. The program at Montbalm is large and serves a population that includes rural, suburban, and urban areas. The university has worked hard to develop partnerships with local schools to ensure that its teacher candidates have opportunities to work in high-quality field experience and student teaching settings.

Faculty at Abernethy University built their program to prepare teachers to succeed on state-mandated competency and licensure tests while learning the most effective ways to teach students to read in low-socioeconomic environments that surround the university's metropolitan area. Many of the teacher candidates there are also first-generation college students.

As you can see, multiple influences determine what will make a program for teacher preparation stand out, to differentiate it from others. There are many effective approaches (and a few not-very-effective approaches), so your choice of a teacher preparation program is a significant one.

CHOOSING YOUR TEACHER PREPARATION PROGRAM—WHAT STANDS OUT?

For a moment, let's take a step back to your choice of program. If you are reading this book but have not chosen a program, you may want to use this section to help you think through which program is the best fit for you. If you are already in a program to prepare you for teaching, use this section to guide your success in that program. Metacognitive teaching begins in your preparation program, and now is the perfect time to start or continue your metacognitive teaching journey by examining the program you joined or want to join.

Effective metacognition requires research. In this case, you want to scour the program's website and faculty pages for information, talk to professors and former students who are now teachers, and review teaching and learning standards.

Search Program Websites

What might you find on a program website? Accreditation information, links to faculty web pages and course syllabi, required courses and field experiences, demographic information about the program's participants, a mission statement, and recent news. Accreditation standards provide you with a framework for thinking about what you might expect from an

Figure 3.1. Link and QR code for CAEP Accreditation Standards

caepnet.org/standards/introduction

effective program. They also provide you with a way to think about what we know about teaching and what we need to learn. In the United States, accreditation is voluntary, and institutions may opt to pursue regional, national, and/or specialized or programmatic kinds of accreditation (Hegji, 2017). The Council for the Accreditation of Educator Preparation (CAEP), a national agency in the United States, is widely recognized for its rigorous peer review process of teacher preparation programs opting into this specialized accreditation. CAEP's review occurs every 7–10 years. A link and QR code to the CAEP Accreditation Standards can be found in Figure 3.1.

Professional teaching standards are often listed on the websites of teacher preparation programs or alignment with standards may be described in course syllabi. While different countries provide slightly different terminology for their professional teaching standards, they are highly similar. Figure 3.2 provides links to Internet sources for professional teaching standards from Australia, Canada, Ireland, New Zealand, the United Kingdom, and the United States. (Canada has two representative entries because their 10 provinces and 3 territories create their own standards and curriculum.)

Program websites may list other specialized standards to which they align, based on national or international professional organizations' recommendations for teacher preparation in that content area. Refer to Figure 1.3 (Chapter 1) for a list of professional organizations. Open the websites for your content areas to search for subject-specific standards for teacher preparation. Some organizations, such as the National Council of Teachers of Mathematics (NCTM), refer to the guiding document for teacher preparation for mathematics teaching as "principles" or "frameworks" instead of standards; there are subtle differences, but for our purposes, we will use the terms synonymously. NCTM and other professional organizations often reserve the term *standards* for the K–12 curriculum.

Talk with Others

Talking to professors, program staff, and former students can guide your thinking about choices you must make to ensure that you gain as much from the program as possible. That way, you are empowered through information about decisions that will influence your career. Questions to ask include:

Figure 3.2. Sources for Professional Teaching Standards in Six Countries

Country	Website URL	QR Code
Australia	www.aitsl.edu.au/teach/standards	
Canada (British Columbia)	www2.gov.bc.ca/gov/content/education-training/k-12/teach/standards-for-educators	
Canada (Ontario)	www.oct.ca/public/professional-standards/standards-of-practice	
Ireland	www.teachingcouncil.ie/en/Fitness-to-Teach/Updated-Code-of-Professional-Conduct/	
New Zealand	teachingcouncil.nz/content/our-code-our-standards	
United Kingdom	www.advance-he.ac.uk/knowledge-hub/uk-professional-standards-framework-ukpsf	
United States	www.nbpts.org/standards-five-core-propositions/	

- What options are there for concentrations in specific fields or specialties?
- What options and requirements exist for practicum and student teaching experiences in schools?
- How much support is available while doing fieldwork in a school?

Use Standards for Comparison

Teacher preparation standards (i.e., accreditation standards, professional teaching standards) described earlier can provide you with a framework for thinking about what you might expect from an effective program. They also provide you with a way to think about what is known about teaching and what you need to learn.

While you are doing your research, your due diligence, think about the answers to the following questions:

- What themes emerge?
- Do you notice that the different sources of information mention "social justice" frequently?
- Does "balanced literacy" appear with some regularity?
- Will you spend time in schools doing fieldwork where you apply theories and techniques learned in your coursework?

Jot your answers down in a notebook or use a note-taking app. Then complete the chart in Figure 3.3 for each program you are considering.

Challenge Your Assumptions About Teaching

Perhaps one essential feature to find in a teacher preparation program is that you will be challenged in your notions of what it means to teach and to be a teacher. By the time you arrive at the door of a college of education, you will have spent a significant portion of your life in school as a student, possibly as a parent of students, and sometimes as a school employee. Darling-Hammond (2006) suggests that teacher candidates often believe that their experiences have taught them what they need to know about how and what to teach. Frequently, we remind the teacher candidates with whom we work that good teaching can mean that we teach the way we were taught, but sometimes dreadful teaching results because we teach the way we were taught. Like most of us, you probably were inspired to become a teacher because you were enthralled with learning and you had capable teachers. The challenge is that you have only your own experiences as a learner as a basis for what you think teaching is and how it should be done.

The ideas and concepts about teaching you bring to a teacher preparation program were developed only through your lens as a learner. As you

Figure 3.3. Evaluating a Teacher Preparation Program Using the 2017 ILA Standards

Program Evaluation Questions	Relevant ILA standard	Your Analysis of the Program
What are the key concepts or most important things you see in required coursework?		
What aspects of the program seem to stand out as signature aspects or features of the program that differentiate it from others?		
Do faculty members know how the courses they teach fit with other courses and fieldwork?		
What aspects of your own background influence what you want to teach and how you learn in this program?		
What literacy and learning theories inform the program courses and fieldwork? Most faculty and syllabi will mention some by name.	*Standard 1: Foundational Knowledge:* Candidates demonstrate knowledge of the theoretical, historical, and evidence-based foundations of literacy and language and the ways in which they interrelate and the role of literacy professionals in schools.	
What instructional approaches are used in the courses (e.g., teamwork, lecture, online, inquiry)?	*Standard 2: Curriculum and Instruction:* Candidates use foundational knowledge to critique and implement literacy curricula to meet the needs of all learners and to design, implement, and evaluate evidence-based literacy instruction for all learners.	
What might you learn about creating an environment in your future classroom that encourages literacy?	*Standard 5: Learners and the Literacy Environment:* Candidates meet the developmental needs of all learners and collaborate with school personnel to use a variety of print and digital materials to engage and motivate all learners; integrate digital technologies in appropriate, safe, and effective ways; foster a positive climate that supports a literacy-rich learning environment.	

continued

Figure 3.3. Evaluating a Teacher Preparation Program Using the 2017 ILA Standards, Continued

What aspects of literacy assessments can you find in descriptions of program courses? Will you learn about standardized assessments and day-to-day formative assessments, too?	*Standard 3: Assessment and Evaluation:* Candidates understand, select, and use valid, reliable, fair, and appropriate assessment tools to screen, diagnose, and measure student literacy achievement; inform instruction and evaluate interventions; participate in professional learning experiences; explain assessment results and advocate for appropriate literacy practices to relevant stakeholders.	
In what ways does the program and faculty encourage you to grow as a professional during the program and throughout your career?	*Standard 6: Professional Learning and Leadership:* Candidates recognize the importance of, participate in, and facilitate ongoing professional learning as part of career-long leadership roles and responsibilities.	
In what ways does the program and related experiences address diversity and equity? What experiences will you have as a result to expand your thinking about diversity and equity?	*Standard 4: Diversity and Equity:* Candidates demonstrate knowledge of research, relevant theories, pedagogies, essential concepts of diversity and equity; demonstrate and provide opportunities for understanding all forms of diversity as central to students' identities; create classrooms and schools that are inclusive and affirming; advocate for equity at school, district, and community levels.	

Web link for this figure:
docs.google.com/document/d/1eP-8KO7cM-C4I8ASNjTOjfqp-GeS27-LEGD4YC193JqSA/edit?usp=sharing

Note. Standards are reproduced with permission of the International Literacy Association from Standards for the Preparation of Literacy Professionals 2017, *International Literacy Association* [Website]. Retrieved from www.literacyworldwide.org/get-resources/standards/standards-2017

engage in learning what it means to be a teacher, look for the opportunities that challenge the assumptions about teaching you brought with you to the program. Some ideas will match your expectations, but often you will learn more about teaching from the experiences that challenge the assumptions socialized or baked into your teaching DNA (Bullock, 2011). As a candidate, you will learn to *think* like a teacher, *know* like a teacher, *feel* like a teacher, and *act* like a teacher as you increase your professional knowledge (Beck & Kosnik, 2017; Feiman-Nemser, 2008; Lenski et al., 2013).

NAVIGATING THE ACTIVITY OF TEACHING

Acting like a teacher implies much more than just the appearance of teaching. Much, much more. We have used the metaphor of canoeing or kayaking down a river to describe the activity of teaching (Scales et al., 2017), and we will stick with that metaphor here because it aptly describes what novice teachers do in many ways. Navigating a river in a small craft is much like teaching, and for student teachers and novice teachers, the waves, rapids, and snags are often poorly marked or even unknown.

Teachers must navigate the teaching waters that include a range of forces. In general, the motion of the river of teaching is toward the goal downriver, but other forces affect the activities of teaching and the choices teachers must make. In your teacher preparation program, look for the techniques and strategies that will enable you to avoid the snags and survive the whitewater, not just those that work when the water is smooth.

Multiple Factors Influence Teaching

Context is king when it comes to teaching because every teaching situation is different. Sometimes practices at a school are different from those learned in a teacher preparation program. At other times, factors such as the school schedule and resources such as textbooks differ. Rules at the school, district, and state levels vary from one teaching context to another. The makeup of the school community, including community members such as parents and civic leaders, differs, as do their needs. The many factors that influence what and how you teach will vary as a result.

Using activity theory (Engeström, 2015), we can visualize what all these mediating factors might look like in Figure 3.4: All those crisscrossing arrows in the middle of the triangle provide a view of how all those factors change and interact in the context of one school or another, one classroom or another, or even one student or another. Continuing with our metaphor of navigating a river, let us look more closely at those factors labeled at the points of the arrows.

Figure 3.4. Factors Influencing Teaching, Visualized per Activity Theory

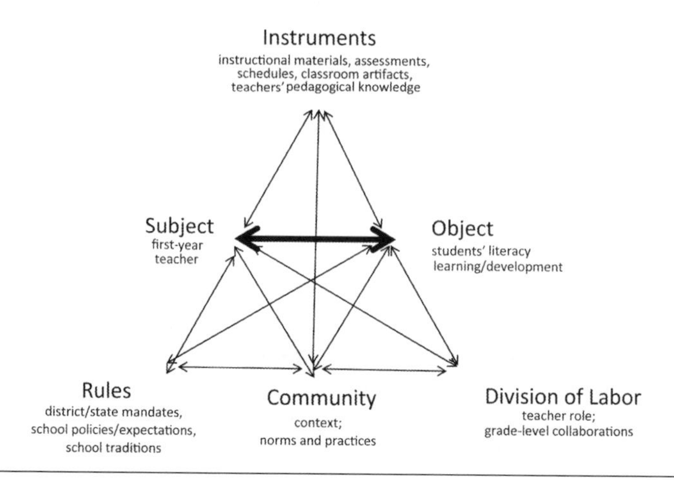

Note. Adapted from *Learning by expanding: An activity-theoretical approach to developmental research* (2nd ed.), by Y. Engeström, 2015, Cambridge, United Kingdom: Cambridge University Press.

The canoeist needs to know what *instruments* are available and what each can do. Paddles, life jackets, and maps are a necessity for any river trip, just as assessment instruments, textbooks, digital technology, and pedagogical knowledge are essential for the teacher. Of course, someone (the *subject*) has to paddle that canoe or teach that class in order to achieve the outcomes desired. For the paddler, that is reaching the destination downstream, and for the teacher the outcome means students who are able and eager to read, write, and think (the *object*).

At the same time, there are certain *rules* or policies that paddlers must follow depending on the river on which they find themselves. Perhaps life jackets are required or a float plan (or a lesson plan in our case) must be filed. Teachers face a plethora of rules about which texts they must use, the pace at which they must teach, and what traditions must be honored at the school. As mentioned above, the *community* or context affects what teachers are able to do. On the water, motorized boats are required to give way to nonmotorized crafts such as kayaks and canoes, but not all of them do. In this case, the community of boaters recognizes that some boats are likely to be less maneuverable on the water than others, so when a member of the community deviates, problems ensue. The wake of a powerboat washing over a canoe is no laughing matter. Teachers, too, must learn what the norms and practices are in their school community, and they need to know what to do when some community members don't conform to those norms.

Traditionally in a canoe, the person in the stern or back of the craft is the one who steers, and the person in the forward part of the boat provides the power. That's a *division of labor*, and it applies in teaching, as well. Different roles exist in education. In some schools, professional learning communities explore how to continually improve their collective approaches to instruction. Often, curriculum is reviewed and approved by district-level committees. Effective teachers also learn how to manage the division of labor in the classroom, too. Consider how students can take on responsibility for classroom jobs to ensure that the classroom runs smoothly and how everyone in the room takes on responsibility for learning.

Hitting the River

As with teaching situations, every river is different. Some have more whitewater than others, and some have hidden snags that change every day. The uncertainty of what lies downriver is often part of the thrill of running a river. Often, the water is smooth, and small corrections with the paddle are enough to stay on course without drifting ashore. Sometimes, the river presents waves and rapids that can knock the canoe over if the paddler is not paying attention or does not have the skills to know what to do in those circumstances. Every once in a while, it makes sense to cross the current rather than just go with it, and every so often, it is even necessary to paddle upstream for a bit.

In teaching, we typically go with the current and avoid any visible snags that might present themselves. For novice and student teachers, a good mentor or supervisor can help uncover the snags that are not so visible and steer clear of those, as well. But there are times when teachers must navigate across the current to avoid a snag or to reach a particular destination. On occasion, teachers also need to paddle against the flow to reach the objective, as well. We will share an example of such a situation later in this chapter.

METACOGNITIVE TEACHING AS KNOWLEDGEABLE NAVIGATION

As explained in earlier chapters, metacognitive teaching means having the ability to make decisions in the moment, in the milieu of all those mediating factors (refer to Figure 3.4) that push and pull, shove and tug, pivot and spin. It also means having a deep reservoir of experiences, knowledge, and skills on which to draw to refine practice and polish professional skills. The goal of your teacher preparation program is to help you develop that reservoir, and to help you continue to refresh it throughout your career. It's from that reservoir that you will draw the strength to know when to float merrily downstream, when to dig in the paddle to avoid a rapid or shoot on through it, and when to paddle against the current.

In our longitudinal study, we examined how the concepts were selected for teacher preparation courses, and how each aligned with other coursework to prepare candidates for student teaching. In an interview with DeVere, university literacy instructor Rhonda explained:

> Well, they came to be key concepts . . . because they're part of the standards for the class and the textbook that was chosen for the class, but more important because they're applicable to the classroom. I tend to focus on the ones that [candidates] . . . can take right into their student teaching experience and use . . . so they can go into a classroom and say, "Wow, I noticed this child's struggling. I'd love to do my case study . . . on this child" and they have had some experience with that. Or if they see that the teacher is on a unit talking about structural analysis, they can say, "Oh wow, I talked about that in my week 2 of my class . . . and I learned that I can use these different strategies for teaching word origins, roots, and structural analysis." So, I guess I would say I came to those based on how applicable they are to the classroom.

Notice what Rhonda said about how she chooses the key concepts to include in her literacy course: She wants her teacher candidates to see the connection clearly between what is taught in the preparation program and what they will see and do in their own classrooms. Gabriela, a professor at the same university, elaborated:

> The key concepts, there are several key concepts. First of all, the fact of what reading is: What is reading? What does it entail? What does it encompass? Really, how does a person learn to read? It's crucial. It's foundational, and I don't think anybody considers it until they come to that class. We all can read. We're all in college. They're all in college. They can read. They never stop to consider what does reading really entail. All of the things that have to happen before a child can be taught to read and all of the different little pieces of reading that are involved, which are so many little pieces. . . . Okay, so that's one of the basic foundational things that I have to teach in class.
>
> Then, on top of that, how do you teach reading then? All the way from phonemic awareness and language and print concepts and all of the outward nonprint foundational work that needs to be done before the child actually encounters the printed page as a process. All of this also has to be taught to the candidate. . . . They're all essential. You cannot eliminate anything.

All those who work in teacher preparation programs and teach literacy coursework feel essentially this way. Reading is such a complex phenomenon that teaching it effectively requires intense preparation and lots of practice teaching it. While Gabriela focused on literacy, each of your university instructors considers key concepts from methods coursework that are essential for being able to teach, regardless of the content area.

Instances of how student teachers understood key concepts from methods coursework appeared throughout case study summaries from our longitudinal research. We noted student teacher Jill's use of literacy teaching vocabulary during an interview. Jill continually looked at her understanding or reservoir of how best to teach by appropriating the vocabulary (paddling with the stream) and by trying instructional routines that expand her abilities. The vocabulary was learned in Jill's teacher preparation program and demonstrates her understanding of key concepts from literacy coursework. The excerpt from Jill's case study summary follows:

> "When I'm *modeling* it [the reading] I'm trying to model the *prosody* and the *intonations* and here's how it sounds, here's how it can sound, here's how it ought to sound when you read. Having the whole group read, it's a way to try to get all of them *engaged*." Jill also stated that if doing the lesson that I observed in her own classroom, she would do it essentially the same way. While she did not give attribution to her teacher education program, she did say [about learning centers modeled in her program]: "I think the centers are great, and they rotate through so the next color group will be at that table tomorrow. It really gives the kids a chance to spend focused time on one activity, but then the next day they spend focus time on a different, possibly related, possibly not related activity. I think it gives them a really broad range of skills. I like it a lot."

In order to be conversant with the concepts and theories of teaching, to know how teachers think and what teachers do, you need to know the terms. You gain this understanding and terminology through your coursework.

Going with the Current

Let's return to the river. In many cases novice teachers just go with the current; there is a lot to learn by doing that. Whereas your preparation program could lay the foundation for your work as a teacher, the actual practices at the school and mediating factors allow you to see what the teaching journey looks like. One key to critical success as a teacher is reflecting on what went on in your student teaching and first-year teaching position and compare that to what you learned in your program.

There are several good ways to implement research-based theory in the classroom. Often, you won't find yourself thinking about the theories while planning your lessons or talking with other teachers. Instead, you will find that the theories and foundations you learned infuse the way you teach. To improve your teaching, take time to reflect on why you do the things you do and why the other teachers in your school context do things the way they do, too.

Consider Steve's thoughts on his student teaching placements about a reading program called Accelerated Reader:

> In both my student teaching assignments in [this school district], the schools have used the Accelerated Reader program to help students choose their reading materials. For most students, this is an excellent way to access reading and to help students build their individual skills. Sometimes this program doesn't work for students that have trouble taking multiple choice tests. I do wish there was another option that could be utilized for these students such as a book report or other book project.

Steve went with the current; most teachers were using Accelerated Reader, and he did, too. However, he noticed that the Accelerated Reader program did not work well for all of his students. A critical stance about teaching suggests that programs, techniques, or strategies that are widely adopted must still be subject to scrutiny: Why is it used? Under what circumstances does it work? For whom? Under what conditions might it fail to work or to work as well?

As a student teacher, Rachel (who discussed using assessments as a novice teacher in Chapter 2) found that her teacher preparation coursework prepared her for a specific framework she would later encounter in the classroom. Her preparation program taught her to use a workshop approach in literacy learning, and when she started student teaching, she found a specific model in use called *Daily 5* (Boushey & Moser, 2014) a framework for daily literacy instruction that includes a workshop component, independent and partner reading, word work, writing, and listening to reading. See Figure 3.5 for an illustration of a workshop approach.

Daily 5 was a new framework for Rachel, but workshops were familiar because of her teacher preparation program. She quickly integrated *Daily 5* into her understanding of what workshops in literacy instruction are and how they work to foster student learning (Young et al., 2017). Rachel said:

> *Daily 5* sort of gave me an actual picture of what a reading classroom looks like, and how to run a reading classroom, and how to handle situations where it's not actually the reading that's the problem; it's the layout and the management and that sort of a thing.

Like Steve, Rachel went with the current. Her school used *Daily 5* and she incorporated her understandings of the workshop approach within

Figure 3.5. Elements of a Workshop Approach for Literacy Learning

Component	Description
Whole-class lesson	Teacher gives brief instruction about a specific skill or strategy.
Small-group or independent work	Students practice the taught skill or strategy independently or in small groups, while reading and writing. The teacher circulates the room and monitors understanding while providing additional teaching as needed.
Whole-class refresher (as needed)	As the teacher determines that reminders about the skill or strategy are warranted, independent and small-group work is paused for brief instruction.
Whole-class sharing	Students gather as a class to share their learning of the skill or strategy. This may be a product or a demonstration.

that specific framework. While her teacher preparation program provided a strong foundation in teaching reading and writing, Rachel appreciated the structure of *Daily 5* and viewed it as a way to help manage her literacy routines.

Encountering Whitewater

Every classroom is a microcosm of life with all the hopes of the society that funds it, the teachers who run it, and the children who learn there. As in life, there are often encounters with rapids and whitewater that threaten to capsize the boat. River runners often shine in the whitewater, and so too do some teachers when they encounter a rough passage. Whitewater on the river and metaphorically in the classroom insists that decisions be made quickly and accurately.

Navigating Around Rapids. Let's take a look at how a novice 5th-grade teacher was able to put context into understanding the real student behind a set of test scores. Georgia, during her first year of teaching, explained to Roya the way Measures of Academic Progress (MAP) tests are used and how to interpret the data. MAP is a computer-based assessment used by many schools around the world. Georgia pointed out students on the data chart and explained their growth in terms of the MAP scores. At the top of the chart Georgia indicated the range of scores that were recognized as average. She then provided examples of question stems from MAP testing related to comprehension and vocabulary, including word origins. Georgia was well versed in MAP testing and quickly rattled off how many students in her class grew in their scores, and by how many points. Georgia stated that she was required to provide a data chart for her principal, which included those scores.

Georgia shared that low MAP scores did not necessarily mean that the reader was struggling. In fact, they could be what she called "medium readers" regardless of their scores. Georgia pointed to a row of scores on the data chart and said, "You can look at her MAP scores and, I mean, even from the beginning of the year to the end of the year she fell 12 points." Georgia went on to share that this was the first year that the student mentioned above had made grades above C, and Georgia called her a "hard worker." She mentioned that this particular student was in a literature circle that Roya had assumed was for the above-grade-level readers. Georgia reminded her that the students in the literature circles were of mixed reading abilities and that the groups were formed by interest rather than by their reading scores. Going with the current would probably have meant that students would be grouped for reading by their MAP reading levels. Georgia chose differently. Instead of going with the current, she paddled around the rapids and formed groups for literature circles based on the powerfully motivating influence of interest (Daniels, 2002; Guthrie & Humenick, 2004).

Navigating Through Rapids. Sometimes the rapids require that teachers navigate through them rather than around, as Kyra found out during her student teaching experience. According to Kyra's cooperating (mentor) teacher, the STAR Reading Test is given once a quarter, and students record their score and monitor their progress. Students also set personal goals for the state reading assessment, administered in late March. According to the mentor teacher, "Starting in January, . . . we started practicing every single week to get ready for the assessments." Much pressure exists at the school to improve scores on the state reading assessment, as the school is on an improvement plan because of low scores the previous year.

Kyra's mentor teacher was reluctant to fully hand over the responsibilities of teaching reading to Kyra until after the state reading assessment. The mentor regularly set aside Kyra's planned literacy lessons to conduct test preparation sessions. Kyra found this practice to be frustrating and tension between the two teachers developed.

Kyra shared in her student teaching interview about taking reading instruction beyond test preparation and about helping students apply the skills to their everyday reading. She said, "We are going over the skills again that we want them to know and helping them as they're reading." Kyra explained that she regularly asked students, "Are you using this skill? When can you use this? How can you use it?"

Different Approaches to the Rapids. Georgia and Kyra navigated the rapids differently, but they both made it through without their boats capsizing. That is, they got through situations that threatened their beliefs about teaching reading without abandoning their beliefs. Georgia used grouping practices for reading groups that recognized her students as individuals who were motivated by choices in reading. Students were not reduced to a numeric score. Instead, Georgia used what she had learned from her teacher preparation program and tapped into students' interests and formed reading groups accordingly.

As a student teacher, Kyra was unable to plan and implement reading instruction without her mentor teacher's approval. Despite the tension with her mentor teacher, Kyra paddled through the rapids with her beliefs intact. Instead of viewing reading lessons solely as preparation for the state reading assessment, Kyra prompted students to consider how they used reading skills and strategies beyond school.

Paddling Upstream

On occasion, it pays to paddle directly against the current. First-year teacher Mia was part of a grade-level team who used cross-classroom grouping for reading. Sometimes she disagreed with the grade-level team's ideas about what was best for her students, even to the point of being subtly subversive. In an interview, Mia stated the following:

> Those kids were all put into my group so that they would have success reading a book, because a lot of them had never finished a book, cover to cover. So, they were put in my group. I would choose books that I thought they would like, would catch their attention, and we'd spend the time reading and discussing. And then those minutes with me would count for their [required reading] minutes. Which . . . Shhh! Don't tell anyone. Because that's not how it's supposed to work! But it's okay because we were reading the whole time, they just weren't doing it at home.

It was likely wise for Mia to keep quiet about how she counted required minutes of reading, which was a school mandate rigidly enforced by the grade-level team. At first she had tried to convince the other teachers but didn't succeed. In this case, she just went about her business doing what she believed would help her students. Essentially, Mia was paddling against the current. Instead of compromising her beliefs, Mia implemented practices in her reading instruction so her students would become better readers.

There is additional empirical evidence of teachers paddling against the current, such as in Seth's longitudinal study on teacher visions. Seth and his colleagues found many instances of teachers "going rogue," where they would do this same sort of subversive thing when it did not align with their vision of what is best for their students (Parsons et al., 2017). Instead of abandoning their beliefs and conforming, the teachers made instructional decisions that were designed to help their students.

Looking for Spaces

Learning how to teach is not easy, and you will encounter many obstacles in your path. Sometimes the obstacles are due to your own lack of understanding, which means you will need to seek help from your instructor, mentor, or a colleague. Instead of capsizing your raft for not knowing, recognize this as an opportunity to look for space to grow. Look for spaces in your routines where you can work toward practicing teaching methods and reflecting on how you can continue to improve instead of trudging through or giving up. You will never know everything there is to know about teaching, so get used to overcoming these kinds of obstacles in a proactive way. Look for spaces where you can try new teaching techniques throughout your career.

One example of a student teacher looking for spaces to grow in her teaching is from Elizabeth. Elizabeth was a student teacher who was, at first, not as prepared to teach as she thought. She looked for the spaces she needed to reflect on and adjust her instruction with the help of her mentor. Mentors can often help teachers at all levels of experience find the spaces they need to continually adjust and improve their practices. Elizabeth often struggled with guided reading, whole-class lessons, writing instruction, and the mechanics of how each worked. She thought of these as activities without connecting them to what students needed to learn and be able to do. Fortunately, Elizabeth had a wonderful mentor teacher who gently challenged her, and Elizabeth rose to the occasion. Her mentor, Betty, observed that writing instruction was an instructional area in which Elizabeth's knowledge was limited, but Elizabeth recognized she still needed to work on her understanding and application of these classroom processes. "She really pushed herself . . . she was having a hard time with writing, so she took on more lessons in writing," Betty said. Through extensive time in the classroom and opportunities to take on teaching responsibilities, Elizabeth and her mentor were able to determine gaps in her knowledge of how to teach reading and writing, and to address these through extensive practice. Betty assisted Elizabeth in her quest to be an increasingly effective student teacher.

Your preparation program provides you with tools and experience leading to the next step in your teaching journey: a classroom teaching position. Often, you will find that some aspects of the school where you work differ in some ways from what you learned in your teacher preparation program. This difference is normal, and it is part of the process. Metacognitive teachers look for spaces where they can apply their knowledge of content and strong knowledge of pedagogy, the *how* of teaching (Snow, Griffin, & Burns, 2005). They learn to anticipate obstacles and challenges and respond accordingly (Malloy et al., 2019). Developing flexibility to work in real classrooms is a disposition that we have found among the successful teachers we work with every day (Young et al., 2017).

Metacognitive teaching requires more than simply navigating your teaching context. We view metacognitive teaching as a never-ending cycle that encompasses many moving parts. While it sounds complicated, you are well on your way to becoming a metacognitive teacher.

THE METACOGNITIVE TEACHING CYCLE

Often, teachers display charts in their classrooms to encourage metacognitive thinking among their students. These charts include thinking stems such as the following:

- I'm thinking . . .
- I'm wondering . . .
- I'm noticing . . .
- I'm figuring out that . . .
- I'm feeling . . .

As teachers, we can use this approach, too. Try it out. Here are examples from teachers we worked with in our longitudinal study:

- I'm noticing that students are more engaged readers when they have choices about what they read.
- I'm figuring out that the scores on the MAP test are helpful, but they don't tell me all I need to know about my students.
- I'm feeling pretty good about the writers workshop today because Farida showed me a draft story that really knocked my socks off (and her peers', too).

Metacognitive teaching can be thought of as a cycle that is ongoing—before, during, and after teaching each lesson. Let's revisit the cycle you were introduced to in Chapter 1. Instead of thinking about this cycle as a step-by-step process, consider it a fluid and ongoing reflection within metacognition teaching because teachers constantly think while teaching. Referring to the four quarters of the cycle shown in Figure 3.6, we highlight what metacognitive teachers do:

- *Plan and teach the lesson, activity, or unit.* This requires thinking about the curriculum standards, what your students know, how to build on their skills, and so forth.
- *Think while teaching to consider successes and challenges.* This requires thinking about what is working well while you are teaching and why it is working, while also thinking about challenges you

Figure 3.6. The Metacognitive Teaching Cycle

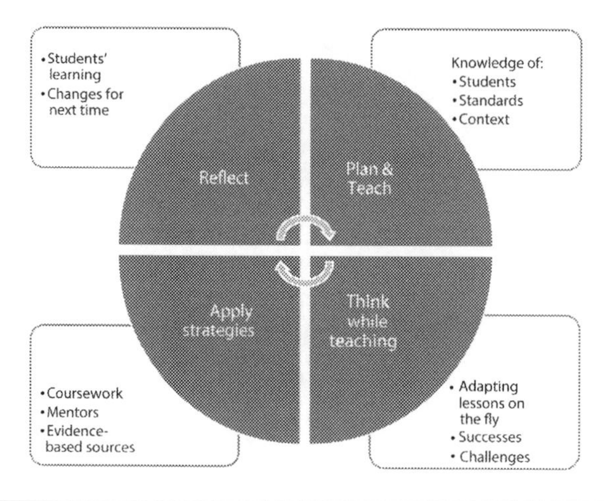

encounter as you teach and adapting in the moment to address those challenges, or considering alternatives for the next lesson.

- *Apply strategies you know from your coursework, those you learned from colleagues, and those you invent.* This requires thinking about and reflecting on the wealth of strategies you've collected and how to use or adapt them.
- *Reflect.* This requires thinking about your teaching and especially thinking about how your teaching influenced your students' learning. Did they learn? How do you know? What do you need to remember to do next time, to build on students' successes while motivating them to want to learn more?

James is a first-year teacher, teaching 4th grade. Let's follow him as he uses the reflection with metacognitive teaching cycle. This morning James taught his students about descriptive writing while also teaching them to attend to the elements of art. He found the lesson on the *ReadWriteThink* website (see Figure 3.7). *ReadWriteThink*, sponsored by the International Literacy Association and the National Council of Teachers of English, features research-based resources that directly connect with English Language Arts (ELA) standards.

During the lesson, students use student-created art and famous paintings to describe in writing what the art looks like. James's students especially liked the matching activity, where they took a partner's descriptive writing and tried to match it to one of the famous paintings displayed on the digital projector. Most of the lesson went smoothly, but not everything did. Let's revisit the steps outlined above and connect them with James's lesson.

Figure 3.7. ReadWriteThink Lesson Plan

Artistic Elements: Exploring Art Through Descriptive Writing	www.readwritethink.org/classroom-resources/lesson-plans/artistic-elements-exploring-through-318.html	

Prepare and Teach the Lesson, Activity, or Unit

James set everything up, preloaded the artwork on the laptop so there would be no connectivity problems, and explained in detail to the students what they were to do. The lesson took two sessions of about 40 minutes each to complete, and students were engaged. In comparing their previous descriptive writing, he noticed that students did a much better job of showing what they meant instead of just telling.

Think While Teaching to Consider Successes and Challenges

Even as students were overall better able to use adjectives to describe the artwork, James noticed that they relied on nouns to get around the idea of description at times. For example, the matching activity was not as successful as it might have been because students wrote sentences like this, "The horse and ox were screaming" (for *Guernica,* by Pablo Picasso). Instead of describing the art using terms associated with line, color, and shape, students simply identified what the subject matter was. Because subjects in the art were named directly, students had little incentive to think about the description.

James had taken a course in his teacher preparation program from a professor who always reminded her teacher candidates to consider the alternatives. What might they do differently, and why might they teach a lesson in a different way? He remembered her advice. Mainly, the lesson on artwork and written description had gone well, but there were alternatives that would improve the lesson in the future.

First, he noted that the directions he gave could be refined, so he wrote in his lesson planner to tell students not to just name what was in the painting. Instead, they should describe using the elements of art, such as line, shape, space, texture, and color. In this way, the quality of their written descriptions would be accented, not just the ability of their partners to figure out what objects or people were in the painting and match it up.

Second, he realized that his professor was right again when she emphasized the value of models. Relying on effective description and not just nouns was a skill that develops over time, and his 4th-grade writers would be better at writing descriptions if they had some examples of good description and perhaps some examples of mediocre description, too (Wolsey, Lenski, & Grisham, 2020). James found a couple of examples from the students' writing, asked their permission to keep them for next year, and filed them away for the next time he taught this lesson.

Apply Strategies You Know from Your Coursework, Those You Learned from Colleagues, and Those You Invent

Okay, so James's plans for next year when he teaches this lesson were noted and in place. But what about his next moves? First, he realized that he could provide models of learning outcomes more often in his teaching. Students tend to succeed when they know what success looks like. Second, James realized that his teaching objectives should align more closely with the directions and instruction he provides his students. These ideas could be immediately part of his next lesson, whether it was on descriptive writing or on inferential comprehension. In each case, he recalled what his professor had emphasized, but now he was able to put those ideas into practice in his own classroom, not just in this lesson but in the next, as well.

Reflect

As James reviewed his students' writing and thought about how he taught the lesson, he considered how his teaching influenced his students' learning. He could tell that students learned, based on his observations of their interactions and their work samples. Their writing indicated that they had learned. Indeed, the students were able to describe in class discussion and in exit slips (also called "ticket out the door"; quick reflection) not just that they had done well, but they could explain why they thought so. Both James and his students assessed the lesson as a success. James also noted what he needed to remember to do next time, to build on students' successes while motivating them to want to learn more. While this lesson was over, James reflected on which teaching strategies and materials got students more engaged because he wanted to continue to use and build on those kinds of experiences in future lessons. His students shared some thoughts, too. They suggested they use the cameras on their phones to take photos artistically that they could then use as a foundation for their writing. As he reflected on this lesson, James was simultaneously considering future lessons. Metacognitive teachers learn from reflecting on their teaching, which shapes their future teaching.

Just as James reflected on his teaching, you will reflect on your teaching. Let's keep James's example in mind as we consider what reflection mean for us all. Reflection, more than just thinking about what happened and what one's opinion might be, is the ability to situate, to identify context, to generalize where context and content intersect. James did that by considering what he knew about his students' learning as he planned and as he taught his lesson. James listened to his students and made adjustments as needed by reflecting on what was happening in the moment and after the lesson by reflecting on students' engagement and their work. Put another way, reflection means having a framework for thinking about what transpired and determining whether the lesson stayed true to that framework, or at least somewhat stayed true. The metacognitive teaching cycle presented in Figure 3.6 is a framework designed to help guide your reflections, and we encourage you to frequently revisit that cycle. It also means knowing the sources of that framework and reviewing them from time to time. For example, in writing this chapter, we reviewed Schön (1983), whose seminal work on reflective practice remains relevant to this day.

Reflecting on This Chapter

- What do you know about teaching literacy and teaching in general? How do you know it?
- Where did you learn what you know about teaching? Can you write about it?
- Often, student teachers and novice teachers are asked to describe their approach to teaching. This is a good time for you to stop and do just that.
  - » What is your approach to teaching?
  - » Whose ideas inform your approach?
  - » What have you read to support that?
  - » What experiences have you had that build upon your approach?
  - » What stands to counter your approach?

FURTHER READINGS AND RESOURCES

Blogs

Calkins, L. (2018, April 23). Advice for launching reading, writing, or phonics units of study.

This post contains practical tips and classroom videos. See how different teachers use the Units of Study approach in their classrooms:

blog.heinemann.com/getting-started-with-the-units-of-study

Newingham, B. (2009, October 17). Reading workshop: What it looks like in my classroom.

Read this post to gain a better understanding of what reading workshop looks like in an elementary classroom. The post features a video so you can see the practices in action. It also provides examples of resources you could use to establish your own reading workshop.

www.scholastic.com/teachers/blog-posts/beth-newingham/reading-workshop/

Schuler, M. (2019, June 12). For the last time, people, teaching is not babysitting.

This post reveals information about teaching that may surprise people who are not in education. Read it and note the items that surprised you. Discuss those items with peers and with your mentor teacher.

www.weareteachers.com/teaching-is-not-babysitting/

Tornio, S. (2016, November 15). 18 clever and hilarious ways teachers define their jobs.

Keeping a sense of humor is essential in teaching. Read this post and consider what you might add.

www.weareteachers.com/teachers-explain-what-teaching-means-to-them/

Videos

Edutopia. (2018, March 14). *Learning walks: Structured observation for teachers.*

Watch this video to consider how you can (1) conduct focused observations in a variety of classroom settings as a teacher candidate and (2) engage in observations as a novice teacher to continue to learn about teaching beyond the teacher preparation program. How can you work with other teachers to build this environment where you learn from one another?

www.youtube.com/watch?v=AUTIIOfma90&feature=youtu.be

Prepared to Teach. (2018, November 14). *Lisa talks about her teacher preparation program.*

This short video features a 13-year teaching veteran discussing the structure of her teacher preparation program.

www.youtube.com/watch?time_continue=51&v=UKZwrawr62s

The Complexity of Becoming a Teacher in University, School, and Classroom Contexts

ANTICIPATING THE CHAPTER TOPICS

- How are K–12 school and college of education cultures the same? How are they different?
- How can you best enter a new community of practice? As a newcomer and guest, what approach should you take to working in a school?

EXPERIENCING DIFFERING CONTEXTS—AN EXAMPLE

In her literacy methods courses, Rosa appreciated and bought into the differentiated workshop model of literacy instruction that her professor taught her. She liked how it embodied evidence-based practice in that it provides explicit instruction for students in individual, small-group, and whole-class situations and also allows plenty of opportunity for choice and authentic engagement with text (Purcell-Gates, Duke, & Martineau, 2007). When she entered her student teaching placement, however, her teacher followed a different model of instruction that was guided by a program with a systematic progression of instruction for the whole class. Small-group instruction was provided, but it was only generically differentiated (i.e., students were in groups based on reading level) and followed a structured regimen of instruction. Rosa was torn. On the one hand, she did not think that the model of instruction that her mentor teacher used was most effective. She preferred a more differentiated and responsive model of instruction that she learned in her university coursework. On the other hand, she was a student teacher at the school—literally a guest in her mentor teacher's classroom. She did not feel that it was her place to question the school's or the teacher's instructional decisions. She was there to learn from them. What should she do?

Situations like Rosa's are not uncommon for teacher candidates in field experiences. Teacher preparation programs and K–12 schools are different entities. Schools and colleges of education are engaged in continuous scholarship exploring the most current and up-to-date research on instructional methods and are guided by theory and empirical research to be innovative and progressive in instructional approaches. K–12 schools have the monumental job of educating numerous and diverse youth to meet increasingly high standards under strict accountability that uses standardized tests to measure student achievement. While generally these entities share a common goal—high levels of student learning for all students—the day-to-day contexts of each differ vastly.

Inevitable Tension

For teacher candidates, it is important to understand this inevitable tension. Indeed, they are caught in the middle of it. Teacher candidates must "serve two masters." That is, they are accountable to the teacher preparation program and professors who are striving to give them the requisite knowledge and experiences to effectively teach students and who are evaluating their progress. Additionally, teacher candidates are accountable to the schools, leaders, and teachers where they complete field experiences because they are guests in the schools. Teacher education scholars have called this dilemma "the two worlds pitfall" (Feiman-Nemser & Buchmann, 1985, p. 63). Teacher candidates operate in two worlds: the world of the university and the world of the K–12 school. Similarly, Young and colleagues (2017) described student teachers' experiences as "cooking in someone else's kitchen."

Ideally, these two entities work together to provide unified experiences for teacher candidates, but it is difficult to do because of the different practices, cultures, purposes, expectations, norms, and limitations of both (Braaten, 2019). School–university partnerships are common, but they vary widely in the degree to which they can embody the ideal unified experience for teacher candidates.

Opportunities for Learning

What is important to remember is that your job, as the teacher candidate, is to learn how to be the best teacher you can be. And you have lots to learn from both your teacher preparation program and your field experiences. Being a metacognitive teacher—one who is knowledgeable, observant, and reflective—will help you maximize your learning. Let's return to Rosa's predicament and see how she handles it.

Rosa has been sure to carefully observe the practices, culture, expectations, norms, procedures, and routines of her student teaching school and classroom. She is proactive in the classroom, taking initiative whenever she feels confident in the task at hand—that is, when she is confident that she knows what her mentor teacher would like her to do in the situation. Rosa is also very communicative with her mentor teacher and university supervisor. She listens carefully when her mentor teacher explains different procedural and instructional decisions, often taking notes to heighten her understanding and memory. She also asks lots of questions to clarify her understanding and to obtain a strong holistic understanding of the instruction, management, and routines in the class. She also communicates frequently with her university supervisor to help her situate her ongoing learning with her previous learning in methods courses. This behavior is representative of being a metacognitive teacher. Rosa is learning as much as she can about the specific context in which she finds herself, and she is considering this information in light of what she already knows about effective instruction from her previous experiences and from her university coursework. She is learning a lot about teaching generally and in this specific class.

Communication

Rosa and her university supervisor discussed the disconnect between her own vision of effective literacy instruction and the literacy instruction taking place in her placement classroom. Her university supervisor urged her to observe carefully and see what she could learn from the instruction taking place and to be careful to not overstep as the intern. "Build contextual knowledge and relationships first," her university supervisor advised. So before saying anything to her mentor teacher, she first gained a comprehensive understanding of the school culture, the classroom culture, and the grade-level curriculum. Once she completed this over several weeks, she decided to talk to her mentor teacher about her thoughts. Rosa consulted with her university supervisor in advance and together they considered how best to approach it. She expressed to her mentor teacher that the literacy program the school uses doesn't align with what she learned in her university literacy methods courses, and Rosa asked how she felt about the program. The mentor teacher revealed that she, too, preferred a more differentiated model of instruction but that the school's leadership had adopted the program and was clear in their expectations that for the time being it was to be followed with fidelity. The mentor teacher expressed that she would like more discretion in her instruction and felt that the program was not best for all students. She did concede that almost all students were growing in their literacy learning, though she thought she would negotiate with the school leadership to tweak the program to be more differentiated after she was more comfortable with it.

It made Rosa feel better to know that her teacher also had reservations about the scripted program. Both Rosa and her mentor teacher were strategically engaging in what it means to be a metacognitive teacher within a relatively restrictive school environment (this varies widely district to district and school to school, but typically teachers have some degree of mandates that they may or may not agree with that they must operate within). They were both taking the time to fully understand the situations in which they were working—Rosa with her student-teaching classroom and her mentor teacher with the literacy program—and thinking about how it aligned with their knowledge of students and pedagogy and with their personal beliefs about instruction. This thinking was laying the foundation for how to act moving forward. For Rosa, when she is looking for a teaching position, she is going to be sure that she asks about the literacy instruction and expectations at possible schools. She knows that she wants to work in a school that does not require fidelity to a specific literacy program for her literacy instruction. Her mentor teacher is going to advocate for adjustments to the required program that gives her more leeway to differentiate her literacy instruction.

Intentionality

Both Rosa and her mentor teacher are acquiring the requisite knowledge about the context and about instruction before taking proactive steps. This intentionality is important. If Rosa came into her placement immediately expressing that the literacy program was ineffective and she knew of a better way, then she would have probably not received a listening ear and would not have made a positive first impression with other teachers. By taking the time to fully understand the context, she showed respect for the teachers and the school. After she had established relationships, developed a strong understanding of the classroom procedures, and showed herself to be a thoughtful learner, *then* she voiced concerns about the literacy program—and it was welcomed, not disregarded, because she had put in the work and demonstrated thoughtfulness. In the following section, we review what existing research has taught us about navigating "the two worlds pitfall" by being a metacognitive professional.

PLOTTING A COURSE IN A COMPLEX CONTEXT

How you can effectively operate within "the two worlds pitfall" or when you are "cooking in someone else's kitchen"? To enable you to do so effectively, we suggest adopting the following six positive practices for metacognitively navigating this difficult and complicated context.

Know Your Stuff

One fundamental prerequisite for all the following recommendations is that you have a solid understanding of standards and of effective pedagogy. To engage in the metacognitive teaching and learning that is required to be a strong future teacher, you must become acquainted with the state and local standards for the content that is expected to be taught at the particular grade level in which you are working, so you know what students are supposed to learn.

At the same time you must learn the content and pedagogy associated with effective instruction through the following practices:

- Carefully reading the assigned readings in your courses
- Thoughtfully engaging in the learning experiences presented in your courses
- Attending and learning from professional development opportunities in your internship experiences
- Using your college library's databases to find out what the research says about particular instructional practices

If you are going to effectively work within the two worlds you currently find yourself, then you are going to have to know your stuff.

We want to emphasize that knowing your stuff means knowing what research evidence has shown us. Popular websites *Pinterest* and *Teachers Pay Teachers* have lots of cute and easy ideas for instruction, some good and a lot not so good, but what we mean by "know your stuff" is that you know what scholarly research has found to be effective in instruction. This is what is being taught in your university courses, and this is what you will find in peer-reviewed research articles in your college library's academic databases. A scholar once advised teachers to carefully consider "which activities are *cute* and which activities *count*" (Roser, 2001, as cited in Serafini, 2011, p. 240). Knowing your stuff allows you to make this distinction.

Learn the Culture of Your Internship School and Classroom

Every school and every classroom (your context) is different. They each have their own priorities, procedures, norms, expectations, interactions, and rules. In short, they each have their own cultures. The culture of a school and classroom are important for understanding how things unfold day to day. Some classroom cultures emphasize relationships, where students collaborate as a class and among themselves to make decisions and engage in learning. Other classroom (or school) cultures emphasize respect and treating other people with kindness. Yet other classroom and school cultures emphasize project-based learning or disciplinary thinking or community involvement or place-based instruction or competition and high achievement. The culture of a school is what is valued, what is prioritized, and what guides behaviors and actions in a specific location (i.e., the school at the macro level and the classroom at the micro level).

Your job, as an "outsider" entering the new context of a school, is to learn as much as you can about the culture, answering such questions as the following:

- What are the routines?
- What are the procedures?
- How do people interact with one another?
- How are decisions made?
- How does communication take place?
- What are the expectations?
- How is feedback given?
- What accountability is in place?
- What are the power structures?

A good first step is to review "the literature" on the school. That is, read the school's faculty handbook. Review the school's website. Carefully observe at a school throughout the entire day to try to answer the questions above and more, such as the following:

- Does the school follow a particular approach to classroom management?
- Does the school follow a particular approach to instruction?
- Do teachers collaborate frequently? What structures are in place to facilitate teacher collaboration?
- Do administrators and school leaders come into classrooms often? Do they provide feedback?
- How often do you work with the literacy coach? What are her priorities?
- Are there schoolwide assessments that are given? What are they? How often are they administered?

We encourage you to take notes as you enter a new school and classroom. What do you see? What do you notice? Figure 4.1 provides you with a sample observation form that can direct your attention to different aspects of instruction in classrooms; use it to record information during school visits and observations.

To fully absorb the culture of the school, and not just your internship classroom, pay attention to out-of-classroom events. For example, what goes on at recess? Spend a day or two in the cafeteria with the kids during lunch. Attend "specials" (art, music, PE, and so on) with them and observe

Figure 4.1. Sample Form for Recording Classroom Observations

What expectations, rules, and consequences are posted? Are they consistently enforced?

What routines and procedures have been established? (Macromanagement)

How does the teacher address off-task behavior? (Micromanagement)

What else do you notice related to classroom management?

What are the various ways students are grouped for instruction?

How does the teacher differentiate for learners with different ability levels, language proficiency, or interests?

Did you see any of the following? Explain the activity and the effect on students.

__Critical thinking
__Creative thinking
__Problem solving
__Authentic learning
__Student choices
__ Active participation
__ Technology

Available for download from:	QR code:
docs.google.com/document/d/1bsZSDQpGqdpzHFw9kMvDU7_bKss3V2yEV32kd_lpnJE/edit?usp=sharing	

(and talk to the specials teachers). Listen carefully during staff meetings. Observe, listen, and talk with teachers during lunch, during planning, and before and after school, but do not engage in gossip (gossip is unprofessional and has nothing but negative ramifications for you and for others). Attend family nights and other after-school community events. Continue to carefully observe and take notes during these experiences. All these experiences will give you insight into the culture of the school and the classroom. Understanding the school and classroom cultures lays additional foundation for you to engage in metacognitive actions. This knowledge will help you make decisions that are best for kids because they align with state standards, effective pedagogy, and the norms of the school and classroom.

Build Relationships with Your Mentor Teacher and Other School Professionals

To be successful as a teacher (teacher candidate or otherwise), it is vital that you build strong professional relationships with others in the school. In the past, teaching was a somewhat isolated profession. You shut your door and taught. Those days, thankfully, are gone. Now teaching is a collaborative endeavor, which has enhanced the work and the instruction kids receive.

Especially as a guest "cooking in someone else's kitchen," it is essential that you build a respectful relationship with your mentor teacher. It is great if you get along personally, but it is not required. If your personalities do not match (i.e., you would not want to meet for coffee on the weekend), that is fine. You can still cultivate a relationship around teaching the students you serve. Building a trusting relationship helps you best learn from your mentor teacher, who needs to know that you are devoted to becoming an effective teacher and invested in learning from him or her. Showing your mentor, and others in the building, that you are a lifelong learner who is knowledgeable, curious, respectful, responsible, committed to kids, and proactive will all lay the foundation for mutual respect, which is the core of strong relationships.

Another fundamental aspect of a relationship is communication. Consistent and open communication between you and your mentor teacher is central to your success in the beginning phase of your teaching journey. Openly talk to your mentor teacher about how and when to communicate. Is texting okay? How late is too late to call or text? Would your mentor like a weekly email summarizing your activities in and questions about the class? We've had some mentor teacher–student teacher pairs maintain a shared Google Doc where the student teacher would draft questions and ideas and the mentor teacher would respond at least once a week. This allowed much back-and-forth without having to schedule a meeting time. However, the mode and frequency of the communication should be discussed between you and your mentor teacher. Everyone has preferences for how they communicate and you need to honor your mentor teacher's preferences.

It is important to note that it is your responsibility to initiate and stay on top of the communication. Your mentor teacher has responsibility for the educations of multiple children and numerous other nonacademic aspects of the job of which you may be unaware, as well as supporting you in your growth as a teacher, while maintaining a personal life. Therefore, it is not your mentor's responsibility to schedule a formal observation, for example. That is your job. We must also note the importance of professional communication. As you develop a positive relationship with your mentor teacher, you may become friends. That is great! However, you should not share personal communications as you would with your friends. Use professional language and professional style in your communications with your mentor teacher and with any person working in the school.

Use Your Resources

As a teacher candidate, you have numerous resources to support you. You have your university faculty, your university supervisor, your mentor teacher, your fellow teacher candidates, and perhaps other supports. We encourage you to use these resources to engage in metacognitive teaching. Bounce ideas off of these individuals. Ask questions. Pose possibilities. Get feedback on lesson plans, units, projects, and activities. If you have a knotty situation at your internship site, talk to your university supervisor, who probably has been around education and the school for a while, so is likely to provide excellent advice. As noted above, teaching is not an individual endeavor, and as a teacher candidate, you have multiple resources to support you in metacognitive reflection about instruction and school-based challenges. Use the resources at your disposal. For example, teacher candidate Brenn explained:

> We [mentor teacher and student teacher] had a group of students who by midyear of 2nd grade were still at a DRA 3 [reading assessment score]. Knowing their end-of-year goals and knowing we had tried a variety of strategies and supports, I reached out to our literacy coach during my independent student teaching time. She introduced new strategies to me and supported me in keeping me accountable in trying them in order to reach the new goals we set for each child. She provided the space to plan, reflect, and reimplement as we kept the end goals in mind.

Respect the Knowledge and Experience of the Leaders and Teachers in the School

The educators who work at your internship school have taken the necessary steps to become licensed teachers in the state in which you work. That means that most have been in the exact same situation as you are currently in. In addition, most, if not all, of the teachers in the building have been evaluated by their school administrators and/or leaders and have maintained their positions due to demonstrating adequate, if not strong, instructional effectiveness—strong instruction is typically why they are selected to be mentor teachers. They have taught more lessons than you have, they have interacted with more children than you have, and they have seen more educational-based stuff than you have. You may not like or agree with every teacher you encounter or learn from, but it is vital that you respect the fact that they have pursued a career educating children and they have done the work, oftentimes for years and decades. This does not mean that everything they do is top-notch. Indeed, we encourage you to critically examine the instruction taking place, but as we expand on below, if and how you voice this critical examination is important. And it requires metacognition—you must be thoughtful and intentional in how you analyze and learn from these experiences.

In your life and in your higher education experience, you are gaining lots of knowledge that will help you be an effective teacher, as mentioned above. Nonetheless, when you are a guest "cooking in someone else's kitchen," it is essential that you maintain the attitude of a lifelong learner. Humility and curiosity go a long way in your internship experiences. This does not mean that you have to keep your mouth shut or uncritically accept everything that takes place in the internship site. It just means that you come to the experiences with an eager-to-learn attitude and that you metacognitively consider what you observe and learn in light of your existing knowledge. It is important to know when and how to speak up and when and how to keep quiet.

Question Tactfully

As alluded to above, we encourage you to ask questions and even push back against practices that you do not think are optimally effective for kids. However, you must first complete the steps listed above and remember that you are still learning. Once you have put in the significant time and effort to prepare yourself, you can question and push back a little against instructional practices that are less than ideal. And even then, you must use tact. With deep knowledge of pedagogy and the school and classroom culture and with strong relationships with your mentor teacher and other professionals in the building, it is still necessary to be metacognitive and cautious when questioning someone else's practices. Put yourself in that person's shoes as you think about the situation and the instruction. Make sure you consider the local context, the state standards, the specific student(s), the content, the curriculum, and so on.

It is vital that you are tactful in how you approach your concern. Couching it as a question and being armed with empirical research findings are strongly recommended. Be sure to monitor your tone of voice so you do not come across as being critical or sarcastic. Saying something like, "I know that our school uses the *This World* science curriculum [fictional], but has anyone ever discussed using a discovery-oriented approach to science instruction?" This style of questioning is nonconfrontational and inquisitive. This sort of question can open the door to conversations about best practice where a student teacher who "knows her stuff" can thoughtfully talk about the research on the practice and how it aligns with standards and student needs. And if the teacher says something to the effect of "No, I love the science program we use," then you can leave it be and know that in your own classroom you are going to explore different ways to teach science based upon the kids in your class.

Cultivating this frame of mind is important in your time learning in a teacher preparation program and in your internship experiences. You will not be able to implement everything you are learning. And, again, you are "cooking in someone else's kitchen," and that classroom is going to run differently than your future classroom will. A metacognitive teacher is able to learn everything possible throughout all of these experiences with an eye toward the future. Consistently ask yourself how you will apply your growing knowledge in your own classroom. As an effective teacher-in-training, you are taking all that you are learning in courses and in clinical experiences and combining it to think about how it might look in your future classroom. This is being metacognitive.

Reflecting on This Chapter

- Before entering your internship site, what can you do to polish your understanding to ensure that you "know your stuff"?
- How can you best prepare to enter your internship site? Can you create a list of "look-fors" and questions to ask?
- Does it fit with your personality to be proactive, yet respectful of your place as a visitor in someone else's classroom? What can you do to prepare for this delicate position?

FURTHER READINGS AND RESOURCES

Blogs

Barr, D. N. (2016, December 28). Essential advice for every student teacher (that we wish someone had told us!).

Read this advice for student teachers from seasoned teachers. Novice teachers can benefit from this advice, too! Choose three of the shared tips to work on this school year.

www.weareteachers.com/essential-advice-for-every-student-teacher/

Connell, G. (2013, December 19). Teachers share our best tips for student teachers.

This post features tips from seasoned teachers in a video and in a free printable list. Compare the advice shared with what you've already read and heard. What are the overlapping themes? Which pointers can you implement in your field experiences and student teaching?

www.scholastic.com/teachers/blog-posts/genia-connell/teachers-share-our-best-tips-student-teachers/

Cox, J. (n.d.). Dos and don'ts of student teaching.

Read this post and consider how you can implement this advice for field experiences and student teaching. The timeline provided shares excellent advice to consider regarding the progression of the student teaching semester. Follow the hot links within the blog post to gain additional tips and resources.

www.teachhub.com/dos-and-donts-student-teaching

Love Teach [Screen name]. (2015, January 14). 7 Habits of amazing student teachers.

As you read this blog post, consider which of the seven habits you've already embraced and which ones you will work toward during this semester.

www.weareteachers.com/7-habits-of-amazing-student-teachers/

Videos

AITSL. (2015, September 28). *Classroom observation strategies: Learning walks.*

Watch this video to learn how one school implements learning walks to support teaching and learning. See how the team explains what they saw from their brief observation. A strength from this type of learning walk is the later debriefing with teachers because they discussed their teaching and students' learning in relation to what the team noticed. One teacher explains how the learning walks help her be a more reflective teacher.

www.youtube.com/watch?v=pjxg6-fxW2Q

BestofBilash [Screen name]. (2009, November 18). *The value of observation in student teaching.*

This 3-minute video features a student teacher describing what he gained from the observation experience in school and a classroom teacher explaining what she wants student teachers to do while they are in her classroom. You can use these ideas to guide your internship and student teaching experiences.

youtu.be/mMMKv9GoADY

Randazzo, L. (2018, June 30). *Student teacher advice, 10 more tips from a mentor teacher.*

This video captures the essence of our message in Chapter 4. As you watch this video, make a list of tips shared. Think about what you've gained from this teacher's perspective and how you can use the information this semester and beyond.

www.youtube.com/watch?v=Le-vc7bPFlw

VBSchools. (2013, July 23). *Learning walks video 2.*

Use the sample observation form from Figure 4.1 as you watch this video of a 3rd-grade teacher's social studies lesson. The video includes a group of administrators discussing what they noticed (the "look-fors").

www.youtube.com/watch?v=T3HaM-NIYzA

Connecting Coursework to Instruction

ANTICIPATING THE CHAPTER TOPICS

- How can you adapt what you learned in your coursework to address your students' learning needs?
- How can you learn from teaching: before teaching (as you plan your lessons), while teaching (in-the-moment), and after teaching (as you reflect on what you taught)?

PREREQUISITES FOR ADAPTATIONS

Sometimes coursework makes teaching sound easy. Learn the standards, assess your students, develop a classroom management plan, plan lessons that meet standards and match students' learning needs, and so on. Easy. Then you enter a classroom and you have 25 wild and wildly diverse children in front of you, many who would rather be anywhere else than in that classroom. That is when you realize you vastly underestimated the complexity and difficulty of teaching.

In this chapter, you will learn how to adapt what you learned in your coursework to address your students' learning needs while being metacognitive in learning from your teaching experiences. To do that, you must know the content that you are teaching well enough that you can make quick, in-the-moment adaptations as you are teaching. This is not easy and requires pedagogical content knowledge (how to teach specific content) and knowledge of students.

Pedagogical Content Knowledge

Throughout your methods coursework you will gain pedagogical content knowledge. That is, you will learn about content from your methods courses while also learning how to teach that content. While you may have a firm grasp on the content, you need to learn the pedagogy so you know how to teach it. Seth relates this story of teaching his daughter to swim:

> I'm a proficient swimmer, and I've been a teacher for almost two decades. But I had a hard time teaching my daughter how to swim. Then in her first swim lesson with a swim coach, I saw him break down components of swimming, like face in the water, body parallel to the floor, arm strokes—each of these different aspects individually. I thought, "That's pedagogical content knowledge!"—to be able to take knowledge of swimming and provide sound, appropriate instruction.

This example shows that someone can have content knowledge and pedagogical knowledge, but pedagogical content knowledge is something different altogether. Let's use a classroom example of fractions. You may already know how fractions work. You may already have a handle on structures of lesson plans (I do, we do, you do) and what good teaching looks like. But do you know *how to teach* students about fractions using appropriate pedagogy? To be able to take knowledge of fractions and provide sound, appropriate instruction should be your goal. You can have content knowledge (fractions) and pedagogical knowledge (how to teach), but pedagogical content knowledge is something different altogether.

Be Fully Present

Many teacher candidates say that they are in a hurry to get through their courses so they can teach. That situation is problematic because seeing methods coursework as "hoops to jump through" means that those teacher candidates are missing the whole point of their teacher preparation programs. They are "doing time" instead of "being there" to learn how to teach. "Being there" means being fully present, being mindful about what you are learning and how it applies to your future teaching. That means focusing on the whole learning experience from each of your methods courses. Our hope for you is that you will be a thoughtful teacher candidate who learns pedagogical content knowledge throughout your teacher preparation program so that you can be a thoughtfully adaptive, effective teacher who genuinely cares about your students and strives to make a difference. That level of thought requires metacognition, and it requires you to remember your *why*—your purpose for teaching.

HOW CAN YOU LEARN ABOUT TEACHING *BEFORE* TEACHING?

Methods courses tend to require that you plan lessons and then teach those lessons to your classmates in the university classroom or to students in a field experience or internship. These experiences provide you with opportunities to directly apply what you're learning in your methods courses to your field experience. As you plan lessons, you are considering expectations based on grade-level standards and how to teach the content, while keeping in mind what you know about students' learning needs.

Talk About Your Anxieties

The content you're teaching may be unfamiliar or feel uncomfortable, especially if it is a subject that you may have struggled with when you were a student. Perhaps you are anxious about "doing it right." Talk with your professor about this and be forthright about your discomfort and anxiety. Your professors want you to be successful, and they are there to help you. Teacher candidate Lexi stated the following about learning from her professors at Cathal University:

> Professors share their experiences and I think . . . we can see ourselves as teachers a little better [through] their experiences. [Professors] make [the idea of teaching] more comfortable. . . . Instead of just lecturing about how one day we will be teachers, and one day this is going to happen, . . . most of them have been in the classroom.

Recognize Professors' Connections with Real Classrooms

Just as Lexi shared, professors are connected with real classrooms. Perhaps they were classroom teachers for several years before moving to the university level. Perhaps they continue to work with and alongside classroom teachers when they are not teaching methods courses. Institutions selected for our longitudinal study included only professors who have had prior classroom experience and who maintain their work in schools, working directly with classroom teachers and their students. For instance, Roya provides literacy professional development for teachers and last semester she taught writing to small groups of 3rd-graders, in addition to teaching methods coursework at the university. Seth teaches methods courses and facilitates a school–university partnership. That means for one day each week, he is in an elementary school working with administrators, teachers, student teachers, and kids. Seth, just like the school educators, is committed to providing optimal instruction to the students in this school, and he provides support by giving feedback to teachers and student teachers, mentoring students, modeling instruction for teachers, and so on. DeVere is fortunate because he has the opportunity to work with teachers and students all around the world. He often introduces teachers and students to new technologies and how to use them. For example, in the province of Huehuetenango, Guatemala, he showed teachers at a private school how to use a remote area "hotspot," permitting them for the first time to access substantial content from the World Wide Web on a regular basis. In Egypt and China and Hopiland in the United States, DeVere learns from the teachers and students about how they learn, what matters to them, and how their culture informs their views of the world.

Collaborate on Planning Lessons

Often teacher candidates spend hours crafting well-planned lessons. Getting the objective, content, materials, procedures, differentiation, and assessment together in a way that makes sense to your students takes a lot of time and effort. Don't struggle with lesson planning silently, because teaching is a collaborative effort. We encourage you to work closely with your professors, classmates, and mentor teacher so you can gather ideas and materials efficiently. Lesson planning requires a kind of writing that may seem awkward and unfamiliar. However, it is a process that gets easier with time and practice. Ask your professors to share lesson plans that are considered good models so you can see what the expected final product should look like.

Utilize Evidence-Based Plans

A quick Internet search may lead you to websites featuring lesson plans, but they may not be based on research (evidence-based). As a teacher candidate, you need to get into the habit of seeking the evidence behind the lesson plans. Just because it looks like a good lesson plan or it leads to a cute activity doesn't mean that it has research to support it. Professional organizations provide lesson plans on the Internet that are aligned with national standards, and they are evidence-based. You can tailor existing plans to your state standards and to your teaching context. See Figure 5.1 for reputable websites that provide evidence-based lesson plans for all grade levels and all subject areas. For example, the website *ReadWriteThink*, used by James (see Chapter 3), is sponsored by two professional literacy organizations and provides detailed K–12 English Language Arts (ELA) lesson plans.

We actively discourage the use of lesson plans from websites that do not provide research evidence to support their resources. For example, *Pinterest* may have cute things, but where's the research to support that what is on *Pinterest* is evidence-based? *Teachers Pay Teachers* is another website that lacks research evidence for their materials for sale. In addition, they may not fit with your curriculum. Our best advice is to stick with free and reputable resources that have solid evidence from research to support their effective use with students. Figure 5.1 provides direct links to such resources.

Be Thoughtful About What Counts

You can always seek out research to add to lesson plans, and we encourage you to do so. Your students deserve excellent instruction, and we know that you can provide them with this by being thoughtful in *what* you are teaching and *why* you are teaching it. The reference librarian in your university's library will gladly help you find research to support lesson plans you find online that don't refer to the research behind the plans. Explain to your reference librarian what you want to do, show them the lesson plan, and ask them to help you find research articles that support what is being taught.

Attend to Students' Learning Needs

As you plan your lessons, you should be thinking about students' individual learning needs, such as which students learn best when they are seated close to the teacher, which students need additional support through advanced organizers, and so on. By attending to what students in your classroom need, you are differentiating your instruction to directly address those needs. While lesson planning, you will learn to anticipate students' responses to the lesson, as well as what to do if you finish your lesson early and have time left over, and what to do if your lesson runs long and you don't finish in the time allotted.

HOW CAN YOU LEARN ABOUT TEACHING *WHILE* TEACHING?

As you teach your carefully crafted lessons, you will find that sometimes students already know the content that you're teaching. What do you do? Do you continue with that lesson, even though they already know it? Or do you do something else? Maybe as you're teaching, you discover that the content is too difficult for students and they're not "getting it." What do you do then? Do you continue teaching, even though no one understands what you're talking about? Or do you take a different approach?

Have a Plan B

Teacher candidates who just want to "jump through the hoops" will keep teaching the lesson, straight from the lesson plan they wrote. Metacognitive teacher candidates will think about *what else* they could do in the moment

Figure 5.1. Lesson Plan Websites Sponsored by Professional Organizations

Content Area	Professional Organization	Website and URL	QR Code
ELA	International Literacy Association (ILA) & National Council of Teachers of English (NCTE)	ReadWriteThink, Lesson Plans www.readwritethink.org/classroom-resources/lesson-plans/	
Math	National Council of Teachers of Mathematics (NCTM)	National Council of Teachers of Mathematics: Activities with Rigor and Coherence: www.nctm.org/ARCs/	
Science	National Science Teaching Association (NSTA)	NSTA, Classroom Resources ngss.nsta.org/classroom-resources.aspx	
Social Studies	National Council for the Social Studies (NCSS)	AFT Share My Lesson sharemylesson.com/partner/national-council-social-studies	
Art	National Art Education Association (NAEA)	NAEA, National Visual Arts standards and other searchable resources to assist with lesson planning: www.arteducators.org/learn-tools/national-visual-arts-standards	
Music	National Association for Music Education (NAfME)	NafME, Teaching with Primary Sources Curriculum Units for the 2014 Music Standards nafme.org/my-classroom/nafme-tps-curriculum-units-2014-music-responding-standards/	

PE	Society of Health and Physical Educators (SHAPE America)	*SHAPE America,* Teacher's Toolbox www.shapeamerica.org/publications/resources/teachingtools/teachertoolbox/Teachers_Toolbox.aspx?hkey=10cff162-c377-4a71-9182-3373635d9626	

instead of plowing through the lesson plan. Perhaps they would even say something like, "I can see that you already know this, so we're going to try something else," before quickly jumping into Plan B, which could be the next step of learning the content that they are teaching.

Switching to Plan B will not be perfect, but teaching will *never* be perfect because you cannot possibly predict *exactly* how students will respond. You can anticipate students' responses while lesson planning, but teaching is a human endeavor and humans can be unpredictable. You could teach the exact same lesson to two different groups of students and you would be surprised to see how different the responses are, just in those two groups. We would rather have you shift to Plan B, however messy that might be, instead of plowing through a lesson plan that's either too easy or too difficult for your students.

Practice Metacognitive Teaching

Making the Plan B attempt is admirable, because it demonstrates that you are being metacognitive in your teaching. You won't harm students if you adapt your lesson. It might feel awkward because you've "gone rogue." If you're worried about doing something wrong by veering away from your well-crafted plans, maybe adapting your instruction will feel uncomfortable at first. Adapting isn't giving up control. Adapting means you're controlling your actions as a reflective teacher, based on what your students need.

Instead of teaching the lesson plan, the metacognitive teacher is teaching *students*. Metacognitive teachers constantly think about their teaching *while* they are teaching and quickly make adaptations during lessons, based on their students' responses. Being metacognitive while you are teaching means that you are learning and growing as a teacher because you are thinking about how your teaching practices influence your students' learning.

Differentiate to Support Students

How can you judge whether students understand what you're teaching while you're teaching? To do that, you must know the students that you are teaching as individual learners. What do they need, as far as teacher support during lessons, to be successful in their learning? Perhaps they need to be near the teacher so they can focus, or perhaps they need movement built into the lesson to keep them actively engaged. A wide variety of learning needs exists, and we cannot predict the ones you will encounter in your field experiences and in your future teaching situations. However, you can talk with your mentor teacher about how you should plan to differentiate your instruction to fully support students' diverse learning needs. Your mentor teacher knows the students from working with them all year, and this guidance is important to consider. How can you support the students who may not grasp the content and struggle during the lesson? How can you extend the lesson for students who grasp the content quickly? How do you meet both those learning needs in the same lesson? Let's think about this quote from Lexi, a teacher candidate in a twice-weekly, 4th-grade internship:

> Every person's internship is different, so the [teacher preparation] program itself is teaching a general idea of what is going to be expected. And then you actually get into the classroom and there are students that can't read yet. Or there are students who are above grade level. So, it is a struggle to individualize all the different readers when you know their background, but you don't know it well enough to provide the resources that they need.

Think Beyond Data

Lexi talked with her mentor teacher to learn about students' learning needs and observed how the mentor teacher differentiated her instruction. While talking with Roya, Lexi said that reading assessment data were important in her placement school for considering how to group and teach students for guided reading, but that her students' abilities went beyond what was presented in the data. Lexi stated:

> I learned a lot from the [teacher preparation] program on how to gauge a student's ability. And that the ability is not just what they can do and what they can't do, but it is more heavily weighed on what they *can* do and *that* is how a student should be measured. I think that it is important for a teacher to tell students that, as opposed to letting them assume that just because they are not in a certain group for reading, they can't do it.

Instead of using assessment data to determine what students lacked, Lexi viewed them as opportunities for growth. As a metacognitive teacher candidate, Lexi thought about how the data compared to what she and her mentor teacher knew about students' in-class performance. She thought about each student as having strengths that she could build on through her intentional teaching.

Help Students with Goal Setting

Lexi and her mentor teacher talked with each student about goal setting. That is, they shared strengths with each student and guided students to set specific goals for learning. Lexi explained goal setting this way:

> I could ask the students what their own goals are first, what they want to accomplish, how they feel about it, [and] why they think it's important. From there, we can create a goal together before they get into something too big. . . . If they don't realize what they are trying to accomplish, they won't be as motivated. If they are a part of the process of creating that goal, maybe they'll be more inclined to want to reach it.

The goals had to be specific and manageable. While "get better at comprehension" is something we want for our students, a more specific goal identifies one aspect of comprehension that students could work on in a focused way. That way, they can tell exactly how they are working toward that goal and they are learning to monitor their own understanding. For example, one goal could be that the student would use the strategy taught in class for determining the main idea and how to explain the supporting details.

Lexi and her mentor teacher used anchor charts to provide visual reminders of how students could use strategies they were taught. *Anchor charts* are reference tools that serve as reminders for students about content and strategies taught in class. The students whose goals included determining the main idea agreed that they would refer to the anchor chart that showed them how to do this. Some students had trouble referring to charts on the walls, so Lexi and her mentor teacher provided them with a copy of the anchor chart to tape into their reading notebooks for quick reference. For more information on anchor charts, see the blog by E. Mulvahill (2019, March 4), "Anchor Charts 101: Why and How to Use Them" (see Figure 5.2).

Utilize Students' Interests for Motivation

Lexi and her mentor teacher tied goal setting to students' interests because they wanted students to be motivated to learn. By connecting their goal with

Figure 5.2. Anchor Chart Blog

Blog: Anchor Charts 101: Why and How to Use Them.	www.weareteachers.com/anchor-charts-101-why-and-how-to-use-them-plus-100s-of-ideas/	

topics that interest students, Lexi and her mentor teacher were promoting learning for a purpose. Lexi said:

> Once you know what they are interested in, it is important to go about using strategies that are best for that individual. So, once you figure out what works and what doesn't work, you need to reinforce the one that does work.

For instance, in Lexi's field placement class, Devin was interested in wolves. During independent reading time, he had access to a variety of books and he consistently chose to read books or other texts (e.g., periodicals, online articles) that were about wolves. As he read about wolves, Devin also worked toward the goal of determining the main idea and how to explain the supporting details that indicate that was the main idea. Lexi and her mentor teacher monitored Devin's progress each week. Devin kept track of how often he used the main idea anchor chart by drawing a wolf paw print on his copy of the anchor chart in his reading notebook. Because Devin loved wolves, this was a great way for him to practice using the main idea strategy, and his way of tracking his use of the strategy made sense for him.

Students tend to be interested in a variety of topics, such as sports, animals, bikes, trains, planets, and natural disasters. If you want your students to be highly motivated in their learning, then make connections to the topics that get them excited as individual learners. See Figure 5.3 for a variety of free, online content area texts that have high interest for students. Many sources include a feature where you can choose a different reading level so you could use the same article with mixed ability groups. You may need to register to access some of the sources, but everything is free.

HOW CAN YOU LEARN ABOUT TEACHING *AFTER* TEACHING?

After you teach a lesson, you may be required to write a formal reflection for your methods courses to explain how the lesson went and what you would do differently next time. The exact directions will be provided by

Figure 5.3. Free Online Texts for Classroom Use

Resource	Description	Website URL	QR Code
America in Class	Primary sources for history and literature	americainclass.org/primary-sources/	
Center for Urban Education	One-Page Nonfiction Reading/Thinking Passages	teacher.depaul.edu/Nonfiction_Readings.htm	
DOGO News	News articles on current events, science, and social studies	www.dogonews.com/	
Library of Congress	Primary source documents arranged by topic or era	www.loc.gov/teachers/	
NewsELA	News articles on current events, science, social studies, and other topics	newsela.com/	
Smithsonian Tween Tribune	News articles on current events, related to math, science, and social studies	tweentribune.com/	
Unite for Literacy	Picture books on math, science, and social studies topics	www.uniteforliteracy.com/	

Figure 5.3. Free Online Texts for Classroom Use

Wonderopolis	Articles providing explanations of math, science, social studies, and other topics	wonderopolis.org/wonders	

your professor. While you may be tempted to see this as just one more requirement (yet another hoop to jump through!), think of reflection as something that metacognitive teachers do every day.

Although they don't have to type their reflections and submit them for a grade, metacognitive teachers constantly reflect on their teaching, without prompting to do so. Metacognitive teachers study their teaching through reflection. That means they think about their teaching and how their teaching influenced students' learning. You can do that, too, by asking yourself questions like these: Did the students learn? How do I know? What do I need to remember to do next time, to build on students' successes while motivating them to want to learn more?

There isn't a specific time or place when metacognitive teachers reflect on their teaching. It could happen while driving home, grocery shopping, walking the track, or taking a shower. Reflecting on your teaching can occur at any time! Some teachers consider it helpful to keep a journal where they reflect on teaching strategies they've tried. During the student teaching semester, Lexi told Roya that she kept all her notebooks from her teacher preparation program's methods courses. The notebooks served as reference tools, reminding Lexi what she learned from her methods courses about how to teach the curriculum. When talking about her reading methods courses, Lexi said that she was especially grateful for the notebooks where she had recorded strategies to use with struggling readers. Lexi said, "I'm glad that I immediately have some frame of reference so that even if I don't remember any other ones, that's a good starting point. I just keep all my notebooks and I refer back to them."

Reflecting on This Chapter

- What have you learned in your methods courses about differentiating instruction based on students' learning needs?
- What have you learned in your methods courses about adapting your instruction in-the-moment based on students' responses?
- What have you learned in your methods courses about coming up with a Plan B when your lesson isn't working?

FURTHER READINGS AND RESOURCES

Blogs

Barrett, L. (2019, August 20). How to do goal setting with your students this school year.

Review this post for tips on goal setting with students. We especially like the SMART goal planning chart with anchor charts. How can you use goal setting in your coursework, in your field experiences, in your student teaching, and beyond?

www.weareteachers.com/goal-setting-for-students/

Baxter-Bateson, T. (2017, March 15). 12 Must-see TED Talks for teachers.

This blog post gives a description and a link for each of 12 videos about teaching. Choose at least two of these TED Talks to watch. As you watch them, make a list of key points that teachers need to know. How will you use this information to shape your teaching?

www.weareteachers.com/ted-talks-teachers/

Captain Awesome [Screen name]. (2016, June 9). My advice to college students on teaching: Do it anyway.

Read this blog by a 7th-grade English teacher and consider how it compares to what you've heard about teaching. Share this blog with your classmates and talk about other points you could add.

www.weareteachers.com/my-advice-to-college-students-on-teaching-do-it-anyway/

Kane, K. (2016, May 2). 17 inspirational videos to help remind you why you teach.

This blog post gives a blurb and a link for each of 17 videos about teaching. Watch a few (or all!) of these videos and think about your "why" for teaching. Why did you choose this career? What impact do you want to have on your students?

www.weareteachers.com/17-inspirational-videos-to-help-remind-you-why-you-teach/

King, M. (2019, June 25). 6 summer reads for teachers.

Check out at least one book recommended in this blog and read it. How did the book stimulate your thinking about your classroom? What changes will you make, based on what you read?

www.edutopia.org/article/six-summer-reads-teachers

Lee, L. (2019, August 28). Writing as a tool for reflection.

Read this blog and consider how you can set aside 10 minutes each day to reflect on your teaching. What format will your reflection take: handwritten or typed?

www.edutopia.org/article/writing-tool-reflection

Renard, L (2019, February 21). How to become a reflective teacher: The complete guide for reflection in teaching.

Read this teacher blog and consider three ideas you can use from the list. Try those three and return to the list to try others. Find what works best for you and adopt those practices so they become a habit.

www.bookwidgets.com/blog/2019/02/how-to-become-a-reflective-teacher-the-complete-guide-for-reflection-in-teaching

Video

Arizona State University, Tempe Campus. (2015, November 18). *Introducing FOH: Faculty office hours.*

Watch this humorous video about the benefits of talking with your professors beyond the class sessions. Consider how you can learn more about teaching by talking with your professors during office hours.

www.youtube.com/watch?v=yQq1-_ujXrM

Negotiating Classroom Complexity

ANTICIPATING THE CHAPTER TOPICS

- What has your journey looked like, so far?
- How can you flexibly use professional judgment to meet your students' learning needs?
- How can you fit all the puzzle pieces together from your teaching journey to be a metacognitive teacher?

THE TEACHING JOURNEY

Nervous. Yep, that first day of school made me (DeVere) really jittery. As a new teacher, I thought I would be more confident. The principal handed me the keys, and I entered the classroom. It was all me, now. No safety net, no cooperating teacher, no professor to bail me out if my first class of the day did not go well. As it turned out, I was better prepared than I thought, and everything went smoothly on that first day of class. The students were also sharing their first day in a new grade with me, and so we began the journey of a school year together.

Keeping It Simple

Not every day went so smoothly that first year, and it won't for you either. Teaching is not as easy as it looks, as you already know at this point in your career. Teaching means keeping it simple, and managing the complex. Here, we have our quandary. For a moment, let's take a bird walk, an SR-71 Blackbird walk, as a matter of fact. The man behind the SR-71, one of the fastest aircraft ever built, was Clarence L. (Kelly) Johnson. You already know one of his most famous axioms, but you might not have known it was Kelly Johnson who made it famous: "Keep it simple stupid."

If you pay attention to punctuation like we do, you probably noticed that there is no comma after "simple," and the reason is that Johnson was not trying to imply a lack of intelligence on those who applied the concept. Rather, KISS, as it is sometimes known, was just a reminder that whatever the Lockheed division known as "Skunk Works" designed should be stupidly simple so that a mechanic, for example, working under difficult conditions in battle could understand the system and effect repairs (see Rich, 1995). Teachers can take their own lessons from "keep it simple": Students are quite capable of complex understanding if the teacher doesn't overthink the lesson design. *Lesson one for your teaching journey:* Keep the design simple, and let the students do the complex thinking. Trust them.

Making Decisions

Even as we recognize how important it is to keep design simple, teaching itself is an exercise in complexity. Consider the choices and decisions teachers must make every day, and every minute. Teachers make decisions constantly, both planned and unplanned. Some estimates put the number of decisions teachers must make in the course of their jobs at 1,500 per day, and that doesn't count decisions about family, personal life, and so on. (For more thoughts on teacher decision-making from Larry Cuban and Larry Ferlazzo, see Figure 6.1.)

Most important, teachers make decisions on the type of learning required by the students (Koedinger, Booth, & Klahr, 2013). For example, does Farida understand the essential ideas of the lesson to the same degree as Juanita? If not, why not? How much feedback should I provide? How much should Farida figure out for herself?

Koedinger et al. (2013) identified several instructional techniques and what they call "dosage levels" (for example, spacing in time of similar learning tasks). They came up with this astonishing result reported in *Science*: "If we consider just 15 of the 30 instructional techniques we identified, three alternative dosage levels, and the possibility of different dosage choices for early and late instruction, we compute 3^{15*2} or 205 trillion options" (p. 935).

We think you're astonished, too, but we know you are up to this decision-making task. Why? Because you trust your students, you trust yourself, and you will continually reflect on what you do and adjust your approaches as you go. Often, we note that our graduate degree candidates tell us that they wish they had known this or that idea before they were teachers; however, just as our students learn and improve over time, so must we. Keep a thumb tack on what you did in past lessons and extend the string to the future. The teacher you are today is pretty good. The teacher you are next year or 10 years from now will be different, and your students will be fortunate to have had you as their guide at every stage of your career. That leads us to

Figure 6.1. Data on Teacher Decision-making

Blog	Website	QR code
Cuban, L. (2011, June 16). Jazz, Basketball, and Teacher Decision-making.	*Larry Cuban on School Reform and Classroom Practice* larrycuban.wordpress.com/2011/06/16/jazz-basketball-and-teacher-decision-making/	
Ferlazzo, L. (2014, February 22). Quote of the Day: Have You Ever Wondered How Many Decisions We Teachers Need to Make Each Day?	*Larry Ferlazzo's Websites of the Day* larryferlazzo.edublogs.org/2014/02/22/quote-of-the-day-have-you-ever-wondered-how-many-decisions-we-teachers-need-to-make-each-day/	

Lesson two of the teaching journey: Keep the design simple, but know that the actual work will be complex.

Recognizing Complexity

Several years ago, researchers noticed that oversimplified ideas tend to backfire in unintended ways. Spiro, Feltovich, and Coulsen (1996) reported that medical students were often unable to describe heart failure because they believed that the human heart was simply all of the component cells and surmised that heart failure occurs in the same way that cells fail. This isn't true because the heart operates with constraints that are more than the sum of its parts. The researchers describe the medical students' difficulty as a cognitive worldview that is reductionist in nature. The reductionist worldview assumes that a whole is the sum of its parts, nothing more or less.

Put another way, let us say that you love pizza, so we give you a package of pepperoni and ask you to eat it. Next, we give you some mozzarella cheese, and you eat that, too. We hand you a bowl of marinara sauce, and you consume that followed by a crust. You have just eaten a pizza, right? Of course not; reducing the whole to its parts does not make the separate ingredients a pizza. Only a pizza, fully assembled and cooked (best when baked in a wood-fired oven!), is that popular food so many of us enjoy. Teaching is much, much more than the sum of its parts, just as a heart is more than cells, and pizza is more than the ingredients that are used to construct it.

Figure 6.2. Sample Checklist for the First Day of Teaching

- ☑ Okay, you have your lesson plans. All set.
- ☑ Classroom supplies—pencils, paper, crayons. Organized and ready.
- ☑ Newsletter for parents. Ready to go.
- ☑ Bus schedule? Yep, got it.
- ☑ Rotation schedule for gym and lunch? Got it!
- ☑ Duty schedule for bus and playground duty? Yes, it's on the bulletin board.
- ☑ Learned all your students' names? Working on it.

Ready to Teach?

If you are like DeVere approaching your first day in the classroom, you found that you have everything in place per your checklist (see Figure 6.2), but you still have butterflies. The reason is that teaching is a monumental challenge and a perpetual exercise in working within a context that is constantly changing. Here is a little secret: On the first day of class every single year, you should be a little nervous. When you are no longer just a bit jumpy about the first day, maybe it's time to go find another career path. The 4th-graders you taught last year are not anything like the 4th-graders you will teach this year. Each school year is a brand-new adventure, and the best part is that you have the chance to work with an entire class of students who have not been in your classroom before (usually).

Tying a Knot, Grabbing a Lifeline

As a student teacher or first-year teacher, you already know the ropes. Your preparation program taught you well, and more important, you learned well. Still, there are times when no matter how well you know the ropes, you also need to know when to tie a knot joining this idea with that one or when you need a lifeline (or when you can offer one). Throughout this book, we have explored together how to move from learning-to-teach to teaching-with-support to being the teacher of record.

Who you are as a teacher candidate or student teacher is vitally important, but once you are the teacher, your role and your responsibilities change. Before we dive into the details of what it takes to deal with all the unknowns that make teaching such a challenge and also such a rewarding calling, let's turn to Shakespeare to provide a little perspective.

In Shakespeare's play *Hamlet,* the lead character is faced with a dilemma. Before the untimely death of his father, he is a prince doing things princes do. But princes are not kings, and with the death of his father, he has to remake himself into a king before it is too late (mostly, for Hamlet, it was too late). We would not carry the metaphor too far; after all, most of the characters in *Hamlet* don't come to a good end, and teachers aren't kings (and most wouldn't want to be!). However, there is a message in Hamlet's story. You can choose to become what you want, or not. As a teacher, you can choose to be the learner-in-chief in your classroom, or not. No longer are you the prince dabbling in teaching; now you must be the king or queen of teaching without a mentor teacher serving as a guide alongside you in the classroom. You may not realize how much you relied on your mentor teacher when you were a student teacher. Reflect on what you learned from your mentor and from your coursework. As a first-year teacher you may have an official teacher mentor who meets with you periodically to see how they can help you, or you may have an instructional coach who serves in that role. Your grade-level teacher colleagues are there to help you, too. Stepping into the role of teacher is what you have prepared for, and we trust that you will strive to continue to grow in your teaching. We encourage you to step into the role of someone who can help others as you gain teaching experience. One day you may serve as a mentor to student teachers and to first-year teachers.

THE ARC OF A TEACHING CAREER—DEVERE'S EXPERIENCES

Teaching is a lifelong endeavor with complications, joys, and sometimes trials. On your journey you will have many experiences, many of which started before you knew you wanted to be a teacher. Maybe, by following my (DeVere's) arc of a teaching career, you might find a model for how you can take and shape your years as a student, the lessons of your teaching preparation program, and your experiences as a new teacher.

Guided by Good Teachers

Throughout my life, I have been surrounded by good teachers. I suspect that is true for many readers of this volume. Let me explain a bit. In your journey to become a teacher, you will likely recognize some of the best guides on your educational journey that I found on mine. Luck, perhaps, has always been on my side, but whatever the cause and whatever the outcome, some of the best teachers I could have chosen entered my life at just the right time.

Recently, I returned from a trip to the mountains of Guatemala. While there, I visited a school where a community of teachers were so committed to the work they were doing with Mayan children that the air around the mountain was rarified.

At the school I observed three things that seem to be an amalgam of how I came to teaching many years before: I had respect from supportive teachers, I learned from inquiring teachers, and I experienced diverse teaching settings. First, everyone at the school respects and cares for the other members of the school community. This quality may be the most important part of my own journey. I don't know if I fostered this type of environment in my own classrooms; I hope so. I do remember that every one of my elementary school teachers, and most of my secondary teachers, knew who I was and who all my classmates were. Who we could *become* was foremost on the minds of those teachers.

Respected by Supportive Teachers

In high school my teachers offered options but never forced solutions. I was and still am a fan of science fiction, so in my mid-1970s-era high school, I signed up for an English course that focused on that genre. The instructor seemed to believe I had some ability with words, and she encouraged me to transfer to the honors class. The event stands out in my mind as a key point in my own career trajectory because Ms. Howard suggested options and recognized what she believed I could do. At the same time, she did not try to force me out of the course; she honored my interest in science fiction. I did not drop the class.

The school I mentioned in Guatemala offers an education to students who have been abandoned, who were abused, or who simply want the choices education can offer in their lives. The students there are in early to late adolescence, except for one young man who could not possibly have been more than 10 years old. The school founder told me that Carlos showed up on the first day of school 2 years previously. Because he wasn't old enough, the school took him home. Not to be deterred, Carlos showed up the next year. Although still not old enough, the school let him in. Half the height of most others at the school, Carlos joins in classes and works as hard as anyone else at the school. He offers a continually warm smile to his classmates, and they, in turn, make sure he can participate in all the school offers regardless of his age and size.

Before I knew I would be a teacher, I learned that good teachers honor their students by listening to them. More than 40 years later, I witnessed the smile on the face of a student who wanted to learn even though he was too young by normal standards. The school and its teachers honored him by believing in his thirst to learn and to be part of the school community.

Carlos and his story bring me to the second intersection of my journey to teaching. Carlos, like all of his schoolmates, wants to learn. Inquiry is a way of life there. You might think I'm exaggerating when I tell you that all the students saw every experience as an opportunity to learn something new. I'm not. Just as important, the teachers, or *maestros,* at the school were equally engaged in learning. They demonstrated for me the heart of teaching; that is, learning something new about teaching or about the world is a characteristic of the best teachers I have ever known.

Learned from Inquiring Teachers

Before I became an "official" teacher, part of my fieldwork in learning to teach involved working with a 5th-grade teacher, Ms. Jackson, who taught me many things. Maybe she didn't know she was teaching me, but I will bet she did. She was fearless when it came to inquiry. A new computer program (keep in mind, this was long before computers were found in most classrooms) did not slow her down. She turned over the learning, and the teaching, to a team of students who explored the program, learned to use it, and then taught her and the other students what the program could do. The program? A statistical analysis program. Her 5th-graders dived in and began learning how the program worked. I was intrigued to watch the students as they proposed possible uses for the program and tried out several in the time allotted. Teachers are learners, not just imparters of knowledge. Ms. Jackson likely doesn't know it, but I know what I learned from her on my journey as a teacher.

Experienced Diverse Teaching Settings

The teacher preparation program I joined was at a college in a rural community. Cultural diversity was not readily visible. To their credit and my benefit, the professors knew that a community can be a place of strength and opportunity. They also knew that good teachers face challenges that are sometimes uncomfortable. For that reason, the fieldwork and student teaching we did extended into our rural community, but it also took us out to neighborhoods and schools unlike any most of our group of teachers-to-be had encountered at that point in our lives.

We worked in urban settings, rural schools, and suburban classrooms. The value our professors placed on diversity of experiences and on the power found in going beyond one's zone of comfort was evident in much of our classwork and, of course, in our field experiences. Looking through the rearview mirror, I now realize that these experiences were not happenstance. My professors thoughtfully planned each one to ensure that we (all my classmates and I) knew we were supported and that we were going to encounter students who were not like us, who lived in places we had only read about, but who attended schools where their teachers cared about them and tried to inspire them. In this book, we introduced you to teachers just starting out on their own journey toward being a teacher. They, like us, did not become a teacher by virtue of a credential awarded at a specific point in time; they will always be on a journey.

TEACHING: AN ILL-STRUCTURED DOMAIN

For the most part, humans like things that are orderly, but not everything works like that. Mathematics tends to be a well-structured domain, as are technical subjects such as computer engineering (this is not to say these domains of inquiry are not complex or challenging). Ill-structured domains, however, don't fit neatly into specific patterns (Spiro, Coulson, Feltovich, & Anderson, 2004; Spiro, Vispoel, Schmitz, Samarapungavan, & Boerger, 1987). According to Spiro and his colleagues, ill-structured domains resist broad generalizations and don't always support hierarchical relations between elements, prototypes are not always informative, features of the domain take on different patterns depending on the context, and higher-order interactions predominate (an "explosion of higher-order interactions").

If that description of ill-structuredness sounds a little like your classroom, then you understand what is meant by teaching as an ill-structured domain. What worked so well last year may not work this year. As we found at the beginning of this chapter, teachers make as many as 1,500 decisions in a single workday. If we follow the logic of Spiro and his colleagues, we can begin to see that teaching is anything but well-structured. Actually, we probably wouldn't want it to be, for it is the challenge of teaching with so many variables that makes the job even more appealing.

Characteristics and Generalizations

What were the defining characteristics of your specific class, classmates, and professor for the first course you took on your journey to becoming a teacher? Were those dynamics the same as in your last course before student teaching? Probably not. A generalization about both courses would be so broad as to be unhelpful or even counterproductive. So it is with our own classes. As teachers, what worked well in the morning with one group of students may not work as well in the afternoon with a different group. As we have already pointed out, to thrive under these circumstances, new teachers need to adjust their thinking on the fly. Perhaps one of the biggest traps to which you as a teacher might succumb is to blame the students. Okay, it is the 20th day in a row that Matt did not bring a pencil, but the only person over which you really have any control is yourself. Give Matt a pencil and go on teaching. If the afternoon lesson isn't going as planned, don't generalize, flex! Note that when we say, "flex," we want you to engage in on-the-fly metacognitive thinking. That is, think about what you know about your students while monitoring the situation and making necessary adjustments.

Hierarchical Relations

We are probably all familiar with the teacher, at least the stereotypical teacher, who stands at the front of the room lecturing while students take notes. One teacher we knew was very clear with his students, "My way or the highway." Students in his class had to conform to the teacher's demands, or else! If we subscribe to the idea that student learning is what matters most, and if we believe that students will learn when presented with clear challenges that invite inquiry, a teacher-driven mode of instruction won't be productive.

The hierarchies of the classroom rightly resist stereotypical hierarchical structures because teaching is a human endeavor that is somewhat unpredictable. Yes, you are the leader of your classroom. However, students do not learn at the same rate. While you will have well-planned lessons where you anticipate students' actions and understandings, you cannot guarantee that your students will completely grasp all the content of every lesson. Some students need more time and exposure, perhaps through additional explanations and practice. Learning itself is rarely linear even if the ideas with which students must grapple progress from one idea to another. We know, for example, that young children learning to read progress in their knowledge of letter–sound correspondences and word recognition in a predictable pattern (e.g., Ehri, 1994). On the other hand, some students progress in their reading abilities more quickly than others. Each case, each student will require something a little different from the teacher and the classroom environment. As you gain experience as an educator, the number of cases or examples that you can draw upon will increase, but in the meantime, avoid expecting orderly progressions in student behavior or student learning. Instead, flex. Engage in on-the-fly metacognitive thinking.

Another kind of hierarchy existed in your coursework. You were a student learning to be a teacher. Your instructors may have shared strong opinions about how content should be taught, such as by using certain materials or particular techniques. You learned a variety of teaching methods from each course so you can continue to build on that foundation. Being a metacognitive teacher means you need to consider how you use what you learned in your coursework. Instead of following along with what the experts (your university instructors) say, base your instruction on what your students need. One example of this is from student teacher John. John's literacy methods professor believed that reading should be taught and practiced through authentic literature. The professor strongly opposed basal reader programs, stating that they were too prescriptive and the stories appearing in the basal were abridged. John understood his professor's concerns, but he learned from his student-teaching experience that basal readers offered some benefits. During a student-teacher interview, John commented about his use of basal readers in a flexible manner and building resources that would engage his students. He believed he had been taught the correct way to do interactive think-alouds in his literacy courses. He appreciated his co-operating teacher who was flexible in the use of the basal reader and viewed the basal as a resource from which to select. John shared:

> I never like just to teach completely from [the basal reader], I like to gather ideas from it and also take what I've learned from [professor's name] and everyone else. So, take a little bit there, it's not a bad thing, nothing's really a bad thing, take what you can get from it and make it positive.

John had freedom to choose which materials he used in his student-teaching context. His cooperating teacher served as a model of how to select from existing resources to address students' learning needs. This experience taught John the importance of being thoughtful about what he knew from experts while flexibly adjusting his use of resources. That is, John engaged in metacognitive thinking because he reflected on how he applied teaching methods that he learned from different contexts and made up his own mind about what he thought was best for his students.

Absence of Prototypes

Remember that fantastic lesson you taught as a student teacher? Everything went exactly as planned, and your students learned and loved learning, too. You considered that lesson a prototype of how to teach that topic. It was so much fun that you tried it again in your first year of teaching, and—yikes!—nothing went as expected. The students did not get it, and their bored looks confirmed that they had checked out. Teaching is often like that. The terrific demonstration lesson from your preparation coursework went so flawlessly that it seemed like that lesson ought to work every time with every class. Until it doesn't.

Step back for a moment and recall a student with whom you worked who had not done well on some assignment. What did you tell him? Did you tell him he failed and he ought to get used to that? Of course you didn't. Instead, you encouraged him, pointed out what he did well, nudged him to try again. We teachers are not always as understanding when it comes to our own important work. What we can do is learn to "fail forward" as we pick up, grow, and move ahead (Will, 2019). You can learn from your errors. One of the best ways to do this is to reflect on the lesson from the standpoint of what you learned in your teacher preparation program and from your experiences after that. You can find colleagues who also have made mistakes and can help you analyze what went wrong, and then grow as a teacher for the next time. Failure and mistakes are going to happen, so just as we expect our students to have a growth mindset (Grant & Dweck,

2003), we can expect that we, too, can learn by failing forward. Go ahead, make some mistakes; your students are more resilient than you might think, and you can learn to engage in on-the-fly metacognitive thinking.

Different Patterns, Different Contexts

In Chapter 3, we examined activity theory (see Young et al., 2017) as a way to situate what you learned in your teacher preparation program within the context of a school that may not do things in exactly the same way as you have come to expect. While you might know a great deal about teaching and learning, the variables you encounter can result in patterns that are not the same as in previous situations. You tell your students how unique they are, quite correctly, but you must also consider the complex implications of how the life experiences, learning trajectories, and demands of school affect what any one of those unique variables (aka students) brings to class each day and how all of that creates interactions with the other unique individuals in the classroom. Different patterns in different contexts mean only that you need to flex. Engage in on-the-fly metacognitive thinking.

Georgia, a new 5th-grade teacher who was introduced in Chapter 3, commented to Roya about taking a chance that a complex text would appeal to her student ("Chloe") who has some intellectual challenges. She put Chloe in a literature circle group to take advantage of the complexity to be found there in a way that would help the student to understand the text. Georgia said:

> She sat and read the book *Earthquake Terror*. I put her in that group because I knew that that text was a little complex, but I knew that she would still work through it because she is a really hard worker. But I knew that she would learn a lot from the people in her literature circle by their talking about what they got from the book, that she would also gain from that. . . . At first, she wouldn't say much during the literature circles, but then she started opening up . . . like "last night I read this," and I think it was a really, really good experience for her, to do those literature circles. She's not the best writer, but I think she definitely comprehends the story. Not so much when she reads it herself, but when people talk about it the light bulbs just start going off, like . . . "oh yeah, that's what was going on! Oh yeah, I remember that happening now."
>
> If you were to ask her what it was about, she wouldn't get it on her own. But by our talking about it, I really think it increased her comprehension skills. I don't know if . . . doing the literature circles got her in the habit of tuning in to what everybody else was saying, but she has really started learning from her peers because of the literature circles. So, she's really doing a good job this year. She said this is the best year she's ever had in grades. This is the first year she's ever made anything above a C. So, I'm pretty proud of that one.

Higher-Order Interactions

Don't confuse higher-order thinking skills, which are important for teachers, with higher-order interactions. These entail multiple actors (e.g., students and their teacher) interacting in such a way that no pair of individuals in the system (e.g., a classroom) can predict the entire nature of the community (e.g., the class; see Billick & Case, 1994). All those decisions that teachers make every hour of every school day are very complex and very dependent on the situation in that minute or second. In the world of the classroom, teachers can become easily overwhelmed. To combat this fog of decision-making, teachers develop routines for themselves and their students.

One routine we highly recommend is meeting your students at the door of the classroom every morning, after recess, and after lunch. This one simple routine can set the tone for your class. No matter what happened at home or on the playground, if you meet your students and welcome them to class by name, they will respond with a positive attitude.

There are several websites and books that can help you identify which routines are needed. Routines make it possible for you and for your students to focus attention on matters of greater concern. To establish routines in your classroom, think about the tasks that are often the major time-eating beasts. Sharpening a pencil, transitions between activities, passing out or gathering papers are all activities that have to be done but that eat up time. Establishing routines and telling students why will help you manage the many higher-order interactions and use your valuable teaching skills in more important matters. Human brains, by design, are seekers of patterns, not followers of rules. You can help your students to focus on what is important by reducing the cognitive load of the small but important tasks to routines.

Learning about what routines your students need could involve something as simple as kid-watching (Goodman, 1985) to make sense of the complexities your learners face. See if you notice patterns in the school day when your students (collectively) seem to need more reminders or have difficulty somehow. Considering those patterns will help with reflecting on your routines and acting the part of teacher as role model.

Reflecting on Routines. Throughout your teaching preparation program and in professional development activities, you probably were asked to reflect all the time. In the challenging ill-structured job of teaching, we can at times let the routines and rules overtake us. Just as we review lessons for effectiveness, we should review the routines of our class. Often, when our students are behaving erratically or are confused, they are responding to a routine that is not working as it should or to a lack of a routine where one was needed.

Some years ago, I (DeVere) shared my middle school classroom with a math teacher, Danny. Danny's class started just after break, and we noticed that the students left their soda cans sitting outside the door of the classroom. We couldn't figure out why, at first, because there was a recycle can just inside the door. After a few days, we figured out the students' behavior was the outcome of following our rule: Don't bring break food and soda into the classroom. Since the can was inside the door, they followed the rule and put their cans just outside the door. Danny and I devised a quick sketch where we hammed it up playing as students trying to solve the problem of soda can disposal after break ended and modeled putting the can in the recycle bin. We didn't have to chew the students out or punish them for littering; we just examined the issue and determined that a new routine was necessary. Voila! Problem solved.

Using routines makes it possible to flex where flexibility is most needed—on learning. Our colleague, Janet, observed a student teacher, Kristie, whose mentor teacher developed a routine to assist her children in choosing books they can and want to read. Notice how Kristie's mentor also built in a way to help students take responsibility for their own reading choices. Janet's case study notes follow:

> According to Kristie's mentor, every child has a book box. At the beginning of the year, the teacher is primarily responsible for placing texts in the box. As the year progresses, the children have learned to select "just right" books, so they select from "tubs of books that are several levels—multi-leveled." Students read daily from their own book boxes. Additionally, many of the students read texts from several classroom collections on an individual basis throughout the day. Once a week, the children also check out books of their choice from the school library.

Acting the Part. While this is not a book expressly about classroom management, a few thoughts fit in well in our discussion of ill-structured domains. Ill-structured classrooms are those that promote inquiry, and that is sometimes messy business. However, *ill-structured* does not mean *ill-behaved.* Sometimes, students do things we would rather they did not do. It's easy to become exasperated, but recall the point we made earlier in this chapter: The only person in the classroom over whom you have complete control is yourself. If you lose your cool, no matter how justified losing it might be, your class will lose theirs, too.

A sports journalist DeVere knows pointed out that he could tell which football teams had coaches who were sportsmen and those who just wanted to win. The coach who ranted and yelled at the referee also had players who did the same. The coach who was a gentleman on the field coached a team of gentlemen players. Class is like that, too. Think about the following classroom situations:

- Students have gotten loud. You yell to quiet them down. Will that work consistently?
- A student tells you that you hate him. You send him to the office. What lesson will he learn?
- One of your students is tapping his pencil incessantly. Across the room, you shout, "Put that pencil down!" Will he put it down? Will other students continue learning if you shout?

Shakespeare to the rescue, again, but this time it's the *Merchant of Venice*. The merchant, Antonio, takes out a loan that if not repaid will cost him a pound of his own flesh, a phrase that now refers to an excessive penalty or one imposed out of spite. Teachers have tremendous power by virtue of their positions and the trust the public places in them. When dealing with a difficult student, usually the less correction you can give is the best. Why yell and disrupt the entire class if you can just gently walk over and put your hand on the tapping pencil. The student will get the message, and you will not need a pound of flesh from a student who probably wasn't even aware of what he was doing. In sum, when a student misbehaves, if you respond with the very minimum it takes to redirect the behavior, the more likely you will be to obtain the behavior you want to promote.

FITTING THE PIECES OF THE TEACHING PUZZLE TOGETHER

Throughout this book we have presented journeys in the ill-structured domain of teaching and drawn lessons for thriving as a metacognitive teacher. At this point we suggest that you look at your own journey and put your teacher preparation program into perspective with your most recent field experiences, student teaching, or first year of teaching. You can use the form in Figure 6.3 to organize your thoughts. Notice that the first column lists specific elements from standards for teachers, based on professional teaching standards from the six English-speaking countries appearing in Figure 3.2 (see Chapter 3). You may want to revisit Figure 3.2 to follow those website links and read about expectations for teachers as professionals, based on standards from around the world. In the second column, you can fill in two or three important takeaways from your preparation program for each area. You need to think about which course or instructor focused on the broad standards mentioned. In the third column, write out your observations from being in a preK–12 classroom and indicate how they differ or match your expectations. In the fourth column, identify an action you can take in one or more areas. Perhaps you will want to more closely align your instruction to what you learned in teacher preparation, or maybe you noticed that what is happening in your classroom is working and you just need to tweak it.

Completing Figure 6.3 and identifying actions that you can take to continue to grow as a professional are proactive steps in your metacognitive teaching journey because this demonstrates your commitment to building knowledge as you reflect on your teaching and learning. We recommend that you keep your completed Figure 6.3 in an accessible place so you can revise and update it each semester. School districts or principals may require professional goal setting based on the state-level or national-level professional teaching standards. Ask your university instructors and mentor teachers about this process. Throughout this book we encourage you to be proactive in becoming a metacognitive teacher as we offer specific suggestions and activities for you to pursue.

Reflect on where you are in your journey of becoming a teacher based on what you have learned from completing Figure 6.3. As you progress through your teacher preparation program and gain teaching experience, you will see how the pieces from your program, student teaching, and novice teaching experiences fit together as you become a professional educator. To illustrate what we mean by this, we asked elementary teacher Joanna to share her teaching journey with us. Joanna explains how she fit the pieces of the teaching puzzle together as she moved from learning in the student-teaching context to becoming a teacher in her own classroom. Joanna's story follows:

> I did my student teaching from 2016–2017 in a 3rd-grade classroom. I was paired up with a wonderful seasoned teacher who allowed me to freely explore and implement curriculum that year. In the first two weeks of school, I spent time writing notes and observations on how she taught so I could emulate her teaching. It felt as if I was gathering the pieces of the teaching puzzle and flipping them over to understand each piece. I sat in awe as students followed classroom rules diligently and established routines quickly. When it was my turn, I knew I had much to learn to become a successful teacher. As such, in order to help myself become comfortable teaching, I cotaught with my master [mentor] teacher. That is when I began to get a gist of what I was doing. Later on in my student teaching placement, I learned that I had to learn by doing; that is, in order to understand how best to teach, I had to jump right in to teaching in the classroom [I couldn't just sit and watch my master teach the whole semester and automatically know how to do it. I observed, but I also had to practice teaching]. I had to learn to be comfortable with being uncomfortable. For example, sometimes lessons do not go as planned and it is important as teachers to modify and accommodate curriculum to students and their needs.
>
> Oftentimes, I would hear my peers in the credential program complaining about writing extensive lesson plans. While I could sympathize, it was on-the-job experiences that helped me appreciate that the lesson plan writing process is designed to help teachers practice developing

Figure 6.3. Reflecting on Standards, Teacher Preparation, and Classroom Experiences

Standard*	Teacher Preparation Program	In the Classroom	Action
Assessment			
Curriculum, Planning, and Instruction			
Teaching all students			
Family and Community Engagement			
Professional Growth and Culture			

docs.google.com/document/d/1Z8nTVdJQ-ev2sReMHZI-w4xZ0_vUXcV5yob210VgLX5I/edit?usp=sharing

*Based on professional standards for teachers from Australia, Canada, Ireland, New Zealand, the United Kingdom, and the United States.

an understanding of the teaching process that occurs on a daily basis. Teachers have to strategically plan lessons backwards for the entire year to ensure that all state standard content is covered, to time manage what and how we are going to teach lessons, to recognize what needs to be retaught the next day if needed, and many other tasks throughout the school year. Although seasoned effective teachers do not always have to write lengthy lesson plans, they have mastered the art of planning and delivering instruction where students are actively learning and engaged. As such, I learned to value the incredible support of my master teacher and team. In many ways, I felt that at the end of my student-teaching year I had finished putting together the border of the teaching puzzle, and developed a strong basis for how to put together the rest of the puzzle.

In the following year as a 4th-grade teacher, I began filling my teaching puzzle with pieces of my previous experiences, support from colleagues, and other research from the master's program at [the university]. I was fortunate to move up with some of my students from the previous year. Early on, I realized that I had to juggle the many different components of teaching: building relationships with coworkers, families, and students; learning curriculum; finding resources; and understanding assessments and grading.

I struggled in figuring out my teaching style and how I was going to present and teach curriculum in a manner that aligned with my own personal teaching philosophy, while also adapting to the various learners in my classroom. One valuable piece of advice that I heard from my peers was to build relationships with my students. Initially, it was hard to learn about all of the different needs, demands, and personalities of 32 individuals. However, after much hard work, it all paid off in seeing the growth of my students throughout the school year. The relationships that I built with my students helped create an intellectually safe and successful learning environment. I am proud of how much my students have grown emotionally and academically.

Although my puzzle is not complete, I am excited to continue to build it as I progress through my teaching career. I am thankful for the experiences I have so far, as there is a clearer picture of what it means to be a teacher. Teaching is like a puzzle that takes patience, time, organization, and commitment to become the very best teacher one can become. [Individual teachers are] . . . completing their own puzzle in their own way, putting together and implementing their own teaching style in the classroom. We must remember that students are also putting together and creating their own life puzzle. Teachers can help students learn the different ways and processes of how to complete their puzzle by meeting the needs of the various learners in the classroom.

Joanna's description of her teaching journey demonstrates her development as and commitment to being a metacognitive teacher. That is, you can see how Joanna continuously reflects on and monitors her teaching practices while adapting lessons based on her students' learning needs. Joanna reflects on her teaching and how she continues to grow as a teacher. Like Joanna, you are on your own metacognitive teaching journey, negotiating the complexity of the classroom. We have confidence in your learning to reflect and adapt as you monitor your teaching and your students' learning as you journey on.

Reflecting on This Chapter

- What do you get nervous about when you think about your first day of teaching?
- Who are some "lifelines" that you can lean on when you have a rough day in the classroom?
- What can you do now to hone your metacognitive thinking that will help you "flex" (engage in metacognitive thinking) in the classroom?

FURTHER READINGS AND RESOURCES

Articles

Rana, Z. (2018, September 15). It's Not What You Know, It's How You Think. *Medium* [Website]. Available at medium.com/s/story/the-trick-to-thinking-clearer-and-better-4a61c54114fa

Read this short article on the role of recognizing patterns in human learning and consider what this means for your teaching journey. How will you prevent yourself from becoming stuck in habit loops?

TeacherVision Staff. (2007, January 25). Classroom routines and schedules. *Teacher Vision* [Website]. Available at www.teachervision.com/curriculum-planning/routines-schedules

Read this short article about establishing classroom routines and schedules. Follow the links in the article to access checklists and other resources. Tailor the list of suggested routines to fit your classroom.

Blogs

Ackerman, C. E. (2019, August 11). Growth mindset vs. fixed + key takeaways from Dweck's book.

Learn more about growth mindset as it applies to adults and children. How can you use this information as you negotiate the complexity of being a teacher?

positivepsychology.com/growth-mindset-vs-fixed-mindset/

Hudson, H. (2019, August 12). 12 must-teach classroom procedures and routines.

This blog provides examples in video and pictures of classroom routines that teachers have found useful. Which of these procedures and routines will you try in your classroom? Remember that not all of these will work for your students. Be sensitive to what your students need and adapt these suggestions accordingly.

www.weareteachers.com/classroom-procedures-save-sanity/

Lee, L., & Merrill, S. (2019, June 20). For teachers, risking failure to improve practice

How do you deal with failure? Read this blog about what to do when lessons flop. Follow the links within the blog to read more and to watch a short video.

www.edutopia.org/article/teachers-risking-failure-improve-practice

Videos

Teaching Channel. (n.d.). *When a lesson goes wrong.*

Watch this video of teacher Sarah Brown Wessling, 2010 teacher of the year, talk about a lesson that did not go as planned. The Teaching Channel's film crew caught it all!

www.teachingchannel.org/video/when-lesson-plans-fail%20/

TED. (2014, December 17). *The power of believing that you can improve | Carol Dweck.*

Carol Dweck shares what she discovered when studying growth mindset and the implications for classroom teachers. How can you use "the power of yet" in your thinking about teaching? How can you use it with students in your classroom?

youtu.be/_X0mgOOSpLU

Your Teaching Journey

Anticipating the Chapter Topics

- How can you continue learning about teaching beyond student teaching and the novice teaching years?
- How do you see yourself as a veteran teacher in a few years?
- How will you plan to keep your teaching fresh and always student-centered?

GROWING IN TEACHING OVER TIME

Working with teacher candidates, student teachers, and novice teachers over several years has taught us a lot about the journey of becoming a teacher. In the last chapter of this book, we want to review what we learned from their journeys to become metacognitive teachers and point out what that means for your own journey.

Teacher Candidates

While every teacher is different, we noticed that growth in teaching evolved over time in our candidates. Teacher candidate interviews captured many instances of "I think," but candidates didn't have much experience at that time. They were taking methods coursework and may have had brief field experiences, such as one day weekly, where they could practice specific concepts as they completed course requirements.

Teacher candidate Ian had completed a few methods courses at the time of his interview. Ian indicated that he knew he had grown in learning how to teach by taking methods coursework:

> I feel like I've learned a lot of stuff that's going to help me be effective, but you're kind of not going to know until you're in the fire. I'm not really worried about it. . . . I've learned to be adaptable and flexible

> and that there's ways to differentiate and all those things. I had no idea about that before. . . . So now at least I feel like I can be successful. When I first came in, I was like, "I'm over my head." There's days that I'm like . . . I have this due . . . I can actually pull something together that would be a good lesson plan [with] a clear objective, [aligned with] standards, and I would know how I was going to assess it. So, I feel like I've learned a lot. . . . I think it's just going to get better as time goes on . . . there's so much going on in everyone's days and lives that you've got to try to pack it in.

We could tell that Ian was metacognitive by the thinking he shared about where he was in his teaching journey. As a teacher candidate, Ian was keenly aware of keeping up with due dates for methods courses. However, he was not focused on simply completing the teacher preparation program (what we've previously called "jumping through hoops"). Ian admitted to struggling at first (being in over his head), but that he grew as a teacher through his coursework and acknowledged that he would continue to grow. While Ian reflected in the interview, he shared that his knowledge was building as he progressed in his program because he was learning about teaching and learning. Ian considered how his learning might be applied in a classroom context, with the anticipation of flexibly adapting instruction to meet his future students' different learning needs.

While Ian was early in his teacher preparation coursework, teacher candidate Sabrina had completed coursework with field experiences when she was interviewed. Just before entering the student teaching experience, Sabrina explained that she had ideas about teaching that were based on her prior life experiences and on her field experiences. She indicated that the field experiences brought the content from the methods courses to life. Instead of simply memorizing content, Sabrina realized the importance of pedagogical content knowledge. She recognized how her teacher preparation program intentionally planned coursework and field experience components. Sabrina's teaching journey made her reflect on what she thought she knew while building on her knowledge from methods coursework. As she reflected, Sabrina considered the adjustments she could make to her teaching in her field experience classroom. Sabrina said:

> While I didn't absorb it all while I was in class, as I go back to look at it now, I'm having a lot of aha moments. "Oh, that's what they meant, I've seen that!" Now as I'm going back and revisiting those particular classes, I'm learning so much more, and I've reflected on what was presented and why it was presented. I'm rereading a lot of the texts. I'm in the process [of] rereading all the literacy texts that we read. It's making so much more sense! I've been teaching, and now I can say, "Let me try this!" Now I understand it. Without that tangible need to teach, you

> know, you don't quite get it all. I'm sure I'm going to be going back to it many times.

Sabrina's comments were typical of the teacher candidates as they were approaching the student teaching semester. The awareness of how methods coursework content shapes actual teaching practices, reflection on teaching and learning from the perspective of the classroom context, and the reality of moving from teacher candidate to student teacher prompted metacognitive thinking. The teaching journey was no longer about passing courses. Instead, teacher candidates gained heightened awareness of their changing roles—their transition time into real teaching. This led to eagerness to learn more, as they recognized that they did not have all the answers.

Regardless of how far along they were in their programs, Ian and Sabrina captured the essence of the teacher candidate trajectory in learning to teach. They both realized they were still putting the different pieces together to learn how to be effective teachers. We hope that you see that in your own journey. Ian and Sabrina shared that they were still learning from the program and from their contexts. More important, their interview excerpts illustrate the metacognitive teaching journey from the outset. Do you recognize your own journey aligning with Ian's or Sabrina's?

Student Teachers

We followed candidates into their student-teaching semester, where they were in a field experience full-time. At this stage, student teachers had completed all methods courses and were working closely with their mentor teachers to plan and implement instruction. Student teachers grew tremendously as metacognitive teachers because they were teaching. Student teachers were thinking about their students and how to build their understandings. That involved planning in anticipation of breakdowns in understanding, while reflecting on methods and teaching techniques that worked for their students and what that meant for the next lesson.

Student teacher Wendy was a teacher candidate when introduced in Chapter 1. Her program required field experiences in the primary grades (K–2) and in the upper elementary grades (3–5). Wendy's interview excerpt below illustrates the message we captured with our student teachers—they learned from courses and from experiences, and they viewed themselves as lifelong learners. Wendy shared how the field experiences and student teaching helped her make sense of the methods course content:

> Honestly . . . this has been a really good placement for me because I have seen exactly what I've been taught the last year and a half. . . . But it's really been good for me to see it in practice because you read about it so much. It's so different when you actually see it and you say, "Oh this

is what they've been telling us about." I think it really is important for us as student teachers or even practicum students that we get a glimpse of what they've been talking about. I . . . really remember reading those things and thinking, "I kind of understand what's going on but I don't really get it." But when I saw it, I was like, "Oh, this really makes sense to me." And I think that's been a big help to me. Just having someone setting that good example of what literacy should look like in a lower grade classroom because I really didn't have an idea. I mean, I got somewhat of an idea [from] my first placement, but it's been a year . . . and I was really worried, coming into a 1st-grade classroom after a year and saying, "I don't really remember everything." And after seeing [Mentor] teach for a couple of days I was like, "Oh, this is what it looks like. I remember this from my classes and stuff. I remember what it should be like." That was really helpful for me.

I feel more prepared now to be able to teach any grade because of the good examples that I've had and the things that I've learned [at the University]. I was really worried when I first started this program. I'm like, "there's no way that I'm going to learn all things that I need to be a successful teacher." I still haven't learned everything but I feel like I'm somewhat prepared to take it on and try being a teacher. I feel like I've learned a lot because of the classes and the practical experiences that we've had. Yeah, I feel more prepared than I did when I started.

Wendy talked about her journey into teaching with explanations of being overwhelmed by how much she had to learn. Perhaps you feel that way too. Wendy understood that her methods coursework prepared her for the content of teaching, but it took pairing content with a teaching context for Wendy to put the teaching puzzle together. Once she saw how the learning from methods coursework looked in real classroom teaching practices, Wendy understood how the different pieces of her teacher preparation program came together. We recognize Wendy as a metacognitive teacher because she reflected on her understanding of teaching and learning in the context of her coursework and 1st-grade classroom, while recognizing that she still had much to learn.

Similarly, student teacher Zara indicated that she was putting the pieces together to consider how to implement reading instruction. Whereas Wendy's student teaching placement aligned with what she learned in her coursework, Zara's did not. What do you do if you find yourself in a field experience or student-teaching placement that does not provide examples of what you learned in your methods coursework? Perhaps you can relate to Zara's experience. Zara explained her thinking, as follows:

[At the University] we learned some great strategies like word sorts and comprehension-building strategies and guided reading in small groups and having them do a lot of independent reading and doing think alouds

> to monitor their comprehension and writing. . . . I don't see any of that in the teacher's manual for [the required basal reading program]. So, I remember it, but that's not what this teacher does, so I need to follow her plan right now. But like I said, I'm learning a lot.
>
> My idea of how to balance all the parts of reading is to have the children reading several different stories at their own level. I know that for some of the children, these stories in the [basal reader] are way too hard. I don't think there's anyone that's beyond that level, but there are definitely kids who can't read it independently or even instructionally. So, I envision having about three guided reading groups where they are reading in smaller groups at their own level. That's more the model we used in kindergarten, but again, we had more teachers in the room. Here we only have the two of us, and usually it's just the one teacher. My question is how to manage that format. You can see that I'm thinking about what I learned and what I'm seeing here and what I'm hoping to do when I'm on my own.

Zara admitted that her mentor teacher implemented reading instruction that was different from what she learned in her teacher preparation program. However, her focus was on learning how to teach reading in the student-teaching context while thinking about her students' learning needs. Zara was metacognitive in her reflecting on the student-teaching experience to build her knowledge of learning about teaching. Indeed, she considered how the context differed from her learning from coursework, but she learned from the context while planning for how she would teach reading in her future classroom.

Novice Teachers

When our student teachers graduated, we followed them into their first year of teaching as novice teachers. Novices talked about getting used to their new teaching contexts, the resources available, how they used what they learned in their teacher preparation programs, and their plans for the next year. Their students were at the heart of this phase. These novice teachers were truly metacognitive because they focused on what they were doing in their classrooms, and their reasons for everything centered on students' learning and engagement. Confidence in their teaching abilities was a recurring theme from the novice teacher interviews. Regardless of how well prepared they felt to teach, novice teachers tended to be nervous about whether they were "doing it right." During an interview with Roya, 5th-grade novice teacher Georgia (from Chapters 3 and 6) shared the following:

> I'm wondering if next year I will feel more confident about [teaching reading and writing], or . . . I'm hoping I will. I know this is because of the new standards. . . . I know that lots of teachers feel just like I feel,

> and whether they've been teaching for a year or 16 years, they feel the way I feel. But I would like to have more of a grasp on what I'm doing and [on] my pacing. . . . I at least want to hit on everything and not completely miss the mark on something. . . . I just really think that I need to grow in teaching. I mean, I really just grasp at straws most days. Well, some days, not most days.

You may feel like Georgia, and that's admirable. Recognizing that you are still growing as a teacher beyond graduation is exactly what we want to happen because that's part of the metacognitive teaching journey. Your teacher preparation program equipped you with excellent understanding of how to teach, but you will never know everything there is to know about teaching. As a metacognitive teacher, you will constantly hone your practice as you reflect on your teaching and on your students' learning. You will constantly seek and gather resources to help with lesson planning, curriculum mapping, and thinking about how to best meet your students' needs.

Roya observed Georgia teaching small groups for reading instruction before the interview, and she noted in the observation notes how comfortable Georgia appeared while teaching, as if she were a seasoned teacher with years of experience. If Georgia hadn't said that she felt like she was grasping at straws, Roya would have never known or imagined that to be possible. During the observation, Roya noted how Georgia flexibly adapted her instruction in-the-moment, based on students' learning needs. As a metacognitive teacher, Georgia reflected on the lesson as she was teaching. She closely monitored students' understandings throughout the lesson by interacting with them, listening to their dialogue as they discussed their thinking with peers, and by observing work products. This careful monitoring further informed Georgia's decision-making as she taught. It is important to note that Georgia's teaching situation was different from other novices because Georgia was hired to teach in the same school where she student taught, so she was familiar with the teaching context.

Watching the progression of teachers as they moved from candidates in coursework to student teachers and to novice teachers was remarkable because we witnessed their development as teachers. Earlier, you met Wendy as a student teacher. During an interview with Wendy when she was a novice teacher, we discovered how she connected the dots from her methods coursework, field experiences, and student teaching. Wendy admitted that she did not understand how all the pieces fit together at first, but she eventually came to realize how everything she experienced and learned from the teacher preparation program was designed to help her teach. Wendy shared:

> I think I understand it more now, being a teacher, than I did back then. Just because we did get a lot of instruction on how to do it, but I learned

> more I think when I was in the practicum or student teaching and realized, "Oh, . . . this is what is going on." I'm very grateful for that realization that I had while student teaching, and then bringing it into my teaching practices. I remember all those things that I'm supposed to do most of the time. I have the other teachers and mentors here that are helping me with "Oh, let's look at this, let's maybe try this." And I think, "Oh yeah, I remember learning about that in my class." I'll go look up the file I have on it or articles I read on it, or books. I still have textbooks that I refer back to and look at and read through to help me get more ideas and just be more confident in my teaching.

Like Georgia, Wendy talked about confidence in teaching and how she is continuing to grow as a teacher. As a metacognitive teacher, Wendy referred to prior learning (course readings and textbooks), and indicated that they made more sense to her as a novice teacher because she was the one teaching. Other supports that Wendy mentioned were the other teachers and her mentors in her school. Metacognitive teachers reflect on their teaching and how they are continuing to learn about teaching. Wendy shared that she was still growing in learning how to teach, within a supportive teaching community.

BUILDING ON THE FOUNDATION

In our longitudinal research, we discovered that teachers who shared ideas and collaborated tended to be more confident and satisfied with their teaching situations. However, every novice teacher shared moments when they were expected to teach a certain way and they disagreed with it. That is completely normal. It's part of learning about your teaching preferences, as well as learning about your teaching context. Wendy explained how her school's expectations for teaching math differed from her beliefs and from what she knew about her 1st-graders:

> Sometimes in math I know that [school expectations] want [the students] to explore more and be more in that mindset where [they] figure it out for themselves. But with 1st grade it's very hard to have them do that and to get the point that I want them to understand. So, it's a lot of guided [practice] and a lot of "Okay, well let's try this instead," or "What about this? What do you think about that?" and just trying to plant a little seed in their minds so that they'll be able to understand [the concept] and get at it later with that.

Become a Lifelong Learner

We cannot possibly predict where you will teach or the grade levels you will teach throughout your career. Your teacher preparation program provides you with a solid foundation, but you must continue to build on that foundation by adopting the stance of a lifelong learner. Wendy said, "You have to think on your toes a lot. Some people have a fear like, 'I wasn't taught this so what am I supposed to do now?'" Given the unpredictable nature of teaching, our best advice is to empower yourself with ways of finding the information that you need, when you need it. Instead of saying, "I wasn't taught this," and feeling lost, adopt the growth mindset mantra of "I don't know this *yet*" and proactively seek the information you need:

- Ask your mentor teacher for help.
- Ask your teacher colleagues.
- Read professional books and scholarly articles. (One novice teacher in our study said that she read 12 professional books the summer before she began teaching so that she would feel better prepared.)
- Search websites that are sponsored by professional organizations.
- Reach out to your professors from your teacher preparation program.

Numerous supports are available to you, but you have to take the steps to find them. See Figure 7.1 for our suggestions of sources to answer your questions. Learning how to seek help will serve you well throughout your career. Seasoned teachers need assistance, too! Think back to Georgia's comments about how 16-year veteran teachers at her school were grappling with the new standards just as much as she was. Regardless of where you are on your teaching journey, know that metacognitive teachers are lifelong learners who learn from a variety of sources. That includes learning from your colleagues.

Draw on Available Support

Novice teachers have different layers of support, depending on resources provided by the school and the district. Wendy taught in a school district in a small city, and she explained the support available from her district and from her school as follows:

> [My] district [provides] classes for all the new first-year teachers. They have them 2 hours, or 3 hours, once about every month or sometimes twice a month, and it will go throughout the whole year. It's just getting

Figure 7.1. Sources for Answers to Teacher Questions

Sources of Support	Teacher Requests
Mentor teacher	I'm not sure what this [process, requirement] means. Could you please help me understand?
Grade-level colleagues, critical friends	I'm not sure I completely understand [this process, requirement, etc.]. Could you please help me think through this? Do you have an example to share, or could I observe you?
Instructional coach	I am trying [XYZ strategy/teaching technique], and it's awkward. Could you please observe and then reflect with me? Can you recommend a model for me so I can better understand how to do [XYZ]? Perhaps observing a peer, attending professional development, watching a video, and/or reading a professional book or article might help me. Could you please help me explore available options?

Available for download from:	QR code:
https://docs.google.com/document/d/11WopoJLjl6edimmL5813Db4KPAHvVycS1gs7XKQW8mc/edit?usp=sharing	

us introduced to new ideas, having us talk with the whole district and everything like that. That's been really beneficial for just . . . I guess getting a new perspective, and thinking about things and not just myself and my other teachers here. Schoolwise, I have a mentor teacher and she's right across the hall from me, which is really good. She's really great. If I have a question or a problem, I'll go to her and say, "Hey, what do you think about that?" She's been a teacher for 26 years I believe, so she's had lots of experience. . . . She gives me her opinions, like, "Well, this is the way you could do it, if you're thinking about it this way. This is how I would do it. This is maybe another way you could do it." She always gives me options of what I could do. Ultimately, it's my decision but I still get that help. . . . The principal, other faculty and staff, really great, really supportive and I just feel like this is a really good school to work at. I love it here.

Georgia taught in a small rural district and was one of two 5th-grade teachers. She taught science and language arts, and her teaching partner taught math and social studies. They switched classes halfway through the school day. Georgia shared that her district provided beginner teacher meetings once monthly. Other professional development opportunities were provided, too. Georgia said:

> I had a behavioral classroom management seminar that I had to attend . . . which was really good. It was . . . a little less than halfway through the school year. There are definitely some things that I tried to implement after that I will definitely try to use next year. We did a thinking maps training at the beginning of this second semester. . . . That is something that our county does, and I know it is pretty big across the state too . . . so I've started teaching those in class. We've used those all year long with our writing, and that's how we've been planning. Whether the kids knew exactly why they were using it or not, they were using it. So, that's one thing that we've had training on. I have gone to a science training on weather. We have a grant in this county to get science kits because we don't really have a lot of resources to teach science. . . . My kit should actually be coming soon. . . . That's about it for professional development.

Despite your context, support is available. Be proactive in asking for help when you are unsure of anything related to your teaching. What might be some signs that you need help? Feelings of being overwhelmed, frustrated, and exhausted are good indicators that it's time to talk. Print out Figure 7.1 and use it as a tool to start those conversations so you can gather fresh ideas and strategies that will help you regain your confidence. Remember, you are on your metacognitive teaching journey, and that's a constant process of learning, reflecting, and thinking while monitoring and adjusting your teaching.

Kindergarten teacher Amber Moss is in her fourth year of teaching. Roya had the good fortune of teaching Amber's literacy methods courses and supervising her field experiences and student teaching. Roya recognized early on that Amber is a metacognitive teacher because she thoughtfully plans instruction based on students' learning needs while adapting lessons in the moment as she quickly reflects on her students' learning as she is teaching. We asked Amber to share advice for teacher candidates and student teachers, for novice teachers, and for mentors in hopes that it will help you along your journey.

> *For Student Teachers and Teacher Candidates:* Learn everything you can from your cooperating teacher! They have so much experience and knowledge. Ask them about their experiences because they have been in

many different grade levels and can tell you what it's like. My cooperating teacher taught 4th-grade and 1st-grade before she taught kindergarten. They can give you some insight if you plan on teaching a different grade level other than the one you are placed in for field experiences. Most important, enjoy it and the students. It goes by super-fast, so take it all in.

For Novice Teachers: Don't be afraid to ask your mentor or any of your colleagues for help and support. They have been in your shoes before and can give you the best advice. The first few years as a beginning teacher can be stressful, but with the support of your grade-level team, mentors, and administration, it doesn't seem as overwhelming because they want you to be successful. Enjoy every moment and take the time to build a rapport with your students. I . . . have students who are in 4th/5th-grade whom I taught in kindergarten as an intern that still come up and hug me in the hallways. Your students will always remember how much you care about them.

For Mentors: Don't be afraid to check in on your beginning teachers from time to time. They may need your support without your realizing it. I know there were times when I was afraid to ask what I thought was a dumb question, but I realized it wasn't dumb at all because I had never done it before.

ACHIEVING BALANCE

A whopping 44% of teachers leave the profession within 5 years (Ingersoll, Merrill, Stuckey, & Collins, 2018). We hope that this book will be a guide for those times when things do not seem to be going well. Return to this guide as needed for reassurance and for reminders. We have always found in our careers as teachers and professors that when things are rocky, we just have to remember all the students we watched blossom in our classrooms. When you are new to the profession, you won't have as many of these experiences to draw on, but you will soon!

What are you unsure about related to teaching? How can you use your resources to find answers? What if you feel lost? Third-year teacher Tori Golden offered this advice:

Find your teacher "bestie." Search for those people in your school that will support and encourage you. As a new teacher, don't be afraid to ask for help and take advice. If you have a chance, observe other teachers in your school. You can learn so much from the teacher next door or down the hall.

Trust yourself. There will be days when you feel like you aren't doing enough or your lesson wasn't engaging enough. You are enough. You have been prepared for this, you have worked for this, and those kiddos are lucky to have you.

Always remember your "why." There will be days when you feel overwhelmed, stressed, and burnt out, but your "why" will help push you through it. Remember the kiddos that need you, who come to school every day excited to see you and be in your class. Be the teacher you wish you had growing up. Take care of yourself, find a work/life balance, because you can't pour from an empty cup and your kiddos deserve the best version of you every day.

Work/Life Balance

What did Tori mean by work/life balance? Have you considered who you are beyond the school setting? Maybe you have family members and you engage in activities with them, such as hiking, piano lessons, and/or sports. Attend their special events and be a fully participating family member. Those papers you need to grade aren't going anywhere, and you can grade them later. Do you have friends who are not in education? Make a point to engage in activities and attend gatherings with friends who are not teachers so you talk about life beyond work.

Do you have a hobby? If not, now is the time to start one! It's important to remember who you are as a person beyond the classroom. Roya recently asked her teacher candidates what kinds of hobbies they pursued. The candidates explained that they were so consumed with coursework and field experiences to the point that they couldn't remember the last time they pursued a hobby. No wonder their stress levels were elevated! Their homework was to figure out a hobby they could pursue. Hobbies could include the arts such as crocheting, knitting, painting, photography, and woodworking. Hobbies could include physical activities such as hiking, rafting, and skateboarding. Roya enjoys rafting, and she loves taking pictures of flowers and greenery while walking in nature. DeVere, like Roya, enjoys photography, and he sails whenever possible. Seth loves to fish, and he enjoys woodworking. All three of us are avid readers and we love to travel.

Self-Care

Besides having a hobby, how else can you recharge your batteries and focus on your well-being? Student teachers and novice teachers frequently tell us that learning the ropes of their school contexts is important, yet exhausting. What are you doing to take care of your mental and physical well-being so you aren't perpetually exhausted? Perhaps you've heard of the term *self-care*. What does self-care mean to you?

How are you taking care of your mental well-being? Perhaps you have calming strategies, such as being mindful of your breathing, using special scents that help you feel calm, or listening to soothing music. Maybe you have apps that help you feel calm. Other ideas include working jigsaw puzzles, coloring, and writing in a journal.

What are strategies you could use to keep yourself organized? Do you make lists? Sometimes a list can get so long that it can cause panic. One strategy could be to make a prioritized list with the expectation that you will accomplish up to three things from that list in the next 24–48 hours. Another strategy could be to make a list by days of the week, so for specific days your goal is to accomplish a specific task per day.

How are you taking care of your physical well-being? Perhaps you have an established workout routine, such as walking, Zumba, Cross-fit, or swimming. If you don't have a routine, it's time to find a physical activity that you enjoy so you can pursue it at least 3 days weekly. Are you drinking enough water? Are you making healthy eating choices?

THE BEST JOB IN THE WORLD

We have enjoyed writing this book, and we hope that you have enjoyed the journey with us and your journey to becoming a metacognitive teacher. Teaching is the best job in the world, we think. Stick with it, and we are sure you will come to agree with us. And, most important, take care of yourself. You deserve it, and your students need you to take care of yourself so that they can count on you.

Reflecting on This Chapter

- How can you continue to learn about teaching beyond your teacher preparation program, as a lifelong learner?
- How will you find out about resources and support available to you in your school and district?
- How will you take care of your mental and physical well-being so you are not perpetually exhausted?

FURTHER READINGS AND RESOURCES

Blogs

Aguilar, E. (2018, December 4). Simple tips for boosting teacher resilience.

Try the tips provided in this blog and make a list of other tips that help you relieve stress. Talk with your colleagues about what works for them.

www.edutopia.org/article/simple-tips-boosting-teacher-resilience

Barnes, P. (2019, May 30). Why I stay in teaching.

Read this blog to gain insight into a 22-year seasoned teacher's perspective about preventing burnout while embracing the learning about teaching process as never-ending. Consider two ideas to use in your own life as a teacher.

www.edutopia.org/article/why-i-stay-teaching

Hill, H. (2015, February 13). 15 Tips from veteran educators for thriving in the first year.

Share these tips with your mentor teacher and see if he or she can provide you with more ideas. Talk about the tips with your colleagues and generate a reminder list for when you need to revisit these tips.

www.edutopia.org/discussion/15-tips-veteran-educators-thriving-first-year

Starr, L. (2002). Advice for first-year teachers from the "sophomores" who survived last year.

This blog provides tips to help you as a first-year teacher. Share this blog with your colleagues and mentor teacher and see if you can generate more ideas, together.

www.educationworld.com/a_curr/curr152.shtml

Venet, A. S. (2014, December 21). 7 self-care strategies for teachers.

Choose strategies from this list that you can try. Share this list with your colleagues and mentor teacher. What are other ideas that you could add to this list?

www.edutopia.org/discussion/7-self-care-strategies-teachers

WeAreTeachers Staff. (2019, June 11). 10 of the absolute best podcasts for teachers.

Scroll through this list and choose at least two podcasts to try. Jot ideas you learn while listening to the podcasts. If those weren't what you expected, choose others from the list to try.

www.weareteachers.com/must-listen-podcasts/

Videos

AITSL. (2012, January 2). *Short version—professional learning animation.*

Regardless of where you are on the planet, this short video rings true. Watch the video and consider how you are a lifelong learner who adapts instruction based on students' learning needs. Think about how you contribute to the culture of collaboration and professional development in your grade level, school, and district. How will you continue to grow as a teacher? How will you continue to learn about teaching?

www.youtube.com/watch?time_continue=162&v=e6ZifjW-ftc8

Edutopia. (2019, August 15). *What's executive function—and why does it matter?*

As you watch this video, think about the implications for you and for your students. While you can implement these strategies in your classroom, it is important that you also implement them in your own thinking about teaching and learning.

www.edutopia.org/video/whats-executive-function-and-why-does-it-matter

Spencer, J. (2017, August 4). *Because of a teacher (a tribute to all of those making a difference).*

Watch this short video and think about a teacher who inspired you. How did that teacher change your life? Think about the teacher you are becoming. You will change lives in ways you cannot imagine. Thank you for being a teacher.

www.youtube.com/watch?v=1UtCgZZeUeI

Supplementary Materials for Course Instructors, Mentor Teachers, Instructional Coaches, and Administrators

CHAPTER 1. EVIDENCE-BASED AND METACOGNITIVE TEACHING: A BRIEF OVERVIEW

Articles

Consider using the articles listed below as required readings and/or as professional resources to assist with planning class lecture notes and discussion points.

Parsons, S. A., Dodman, S. L., & Burrowbridge, S. C. (2013). Broadening the view of differentiated instruction. *Phi Delta Kappan, 95*(1), 38–42.

Parsons, S. A., Vaughn, M., Malloy, J. A., & Pierczynski, M. (2017). The development of teachers' visions from preservice to their first years teaching: A longitudinal study. *Teaching and Teacher Education, 64*, 12–25. doi:10.1016/j.tate.2017.01.018

Vaughn, M., Parsons, S. A., Burrowbridge, S. C., Weesner, J., & Taylor, L. (2016). In their own words: Teachers' reflections on adaptability. *Theory Into Practice, 55*(3), 259–266. doi:10.1080.00405841.2016.1173993

Vaughn, M., Parsons, S. A., Gallagher, M., & Branen, J. (2016). Teachers' adaptive instruction supporting students' literacy learning. *The Reading Teacher, 69*, 539–547. doi:10.1002/trtr.1426

Blogs

Edutopia. (n.d.). New teachers.

Edutopia, a well-known website with continually updated blog entries, curates a collection of posts of interest to new teachers.

www.edutopia.org/topic/new-teachers

Racines, D. (2019, August 23). 4 Tips for instructional coaches.

While this blog is written for instructional coaches, it provides excellent information for anyone working with teacher candidates, novice teachers, and veteran teachers. Facilitating learning about teaching at any experience level is important. Mentor teachers, university faculty, instructional coaches, and administrators should read this blog and think about how it relates to their work with teachers at all levels.

www.edutopia.org/article/4-tips-instructional-coaches

Teaching Channel. (n.d.). What is coaching?

In your role as an instructor, mentor, coach, or administrator, you work with teachers and teacher candidates. Read this blog and explore the links to watch videos, read articles and other blogs, and view additional resources. Consider how you can incorporate these practices in your work with teachers and teacher candidates to help them reflect on their practices.

www.teachingchannel.org/coaching2

Wolpert-Gawron, H. (2018, March 27). Every teacher needs a mentor.

Read this brief blog post and think about your own experiences as a teacher candidate and novice teacher. Do you remember your mentors who guided you along the way? Regardless of your role, you are working with teachers and teacher candidates. How can you use information from this blog to strengthen the mentoring you provide?

www.edutopia.org/article/every-teacher-needs-mentor

Videos

Nebraska Loves Public Schools. (2017, May 22). *Collaborating for kids: Professional learning communities.*

Watch this short video and consider how you can build or enhance professional learning communities with teachers of all experience bands: teacher candidates through veteran teachers. Think about how you, as an instructor, mentor, coach, or administrator, can facilitate professional learning communities in this way to strengthen teaching practices while maintaining focus on students' learning.

www.youtube.com/watch?v=053ayc0QaeI

CHAPTER 2. METACOGNITIVE PRACTICE FROM STUDENT TEACHING TO NOVICE TEACHING: FITTING THE PIECES TOGETHER

Articles

Consider using the articles listed below as required readings and/or as professional resources to assist with planning class lecture notes and discussion points.

Griffith, R., Bauml, M., & Barksdale, B. (2015). In-the-moment teaching decisions in primary grade reading: The role of context and teacher knowledge. *Journal of Research in Childhood Education*, *29*(4), 444–457. doi:10.1080/02568543.2015.1073202

Griffith, R., Massey, D., & Atkinson, T. (2013). Examining the forces that guide teaching decisions. *Reading Horizons*, *52*(4), 305–332.

Vaughn, M., & Parsons, S. A. (2013). Adaptive teachers as innovators: Instructional adaptations opening spaces for enhanced literacy learning. *Language Arts*, *91*, 81–93.

Vaughn, M., & Parsons, S. A. (Eds.). (2016). Adaptive teaching: Theoretical implications for practice [Special issue]. *Theory Into Practice*, *55*(3).

Vaughn, M., Parsons, S. A., Gallagher, M., & Branen, J. (2016). Teachers' adaptive instruction supporting students' literacy learning. *The Reading Teacher*, *69*(5) 539–547. doi:10.1002/trtr.1426

Blogs

Konen, J. (2018, January 19). 5 questions to tackle when reflecting on teaching.

Consider using aspects from this blog in class sessions with teacher candidates, mentor teachers, and novice teachers to promote reflection for metacognitive teaching.

www.teacher.org/daily/reflecting-teaching/

Moffitt, G. (2019, August 1).Why my practice is data-informed, but student-driven.

Teacher candidates, student teachers, and teachers sometimes believe that test score data is what shapes their teaching. Think about using this short blog as a discussion starter for a larger conversation on how teachers must consider the whole child and not simply reduce them to a number.

www.teacher2teacher.education/2019/08/01/why-my-practice-is-data-informed-but-student-driven/

Videos

Ashby, G. (2017, September 25). *The remarkable learning abilities of the human brain.*

Because teachers are learners and because they work with students who are learning new skills and tasks, this overview might spark discussion about how humans learn.

www.youtube.com/watch?v=73fw0PWU-4U

Edutopia. (2015, August 11). *Morning meetings: Creating a safe space for learning.*

Consider using this video to generate ideas about how to build classroom community, regardless of grade level. Discussion could include developmentally appropriate ways of fostering a positive classroom climate, with attention to necessary components, what that would look like, and what that would sound like.

www.youtube.com/watch?v=iMctALPpLF4

TED. (2013, April). *Grit: The power of passion and perseverance | Angela Lee Duckworth | TED Talks Education.*

This video could be used to prompt discussion about how teachers need to have what Angela Duckworth calls "grit" to persevere in teaching when they are faced with challenges.

www.ted.com/talks/angela_lee_duckworth_grit_ the_power_of_passion_and_perseverance

CHAPTER 3. FOCUSING ON COURSEWORK FOR PROFESSIONAL BACKGROUND KNOWLEDGE

Blogs

Greene, P. (2014, September 5). The hard part.

Consider reading this with your teacher candidates, student teachers, novice teachers, and mentor teachers. What rings true? What are other "hard parts" that could be added to this blog?

www.huffpost.com/entry/the-hardest-part-teaching_b_5554448?guccounter=1

Hopkins, E. (2017, April 3). 8 habits of happy teachers.

Explore this blog and the links within the blog. Consider sharing salient points with teacher candidates, student teachers, and novice teachers. What are other habits to add to this list?

www.weareteachers.com/happy-teachers/

Knoll, J. (2017, April 11). I almost quit teaching my first year. Twenty years in, I love my job. Here's what changed.

Share this blog in class and discuss the implications. What can teacher candidates learn from this teacher? What are the key points that teachers need to remember?

www.weareteachers.com/quit-teaching/

Strauss, V. (2013, December 27). How hard is teaching?

This blog presents answers to the title question. Think about how to use the quotes presented in this blog in your class sessions. One idea is to share one quote per session. Another idea is to present the quotes as an assigned reading and discuss them as a whole.

www.washingtonpost.com/news/answer-sheet/wp/2013/12/27/how-hard-is-teaching/?noredirect=on

WeAreTeachers Staff. (2012, June 15). How to get along with any teaching colleague.

Teachers collaborate in lesson planning, curriculum mapping, professional learning communities, and in other contexts. Consider sharing this blog and think with your candidates about how to use this information to avoid conflict while learning how to collaborate.

www.weareteachers.com/how-to-get-along-with-any-teaching-colleague-2/

Videos

Edutopia. (2017, October 27). *Making sure each child is known.*

Watch this short video with your teacher candidates or with novice teachers and generate ideas together about how they can truly get to know each of their students as individuals. Discuss how making these connections has implications for their teaching and how they impact students' learning experiences.

youtu.be/xjZx0VdmgkE

TEDx. (2018, April 110. *The one thing all great teachers do | Nick Fuhrman | TEDxUGA.*

Consider watching this video with teacher candidates or with novice teachers and discuss how they can: (1) make the most of teachable moments, (2) recognize and appreciate diversity, (3) provide feedback, (4) reflect on and adjust teaching practices, and (5) see students as individuals beyond test scores.

www.youtube.com/watch?v=WwTpfVQgkU0

CHAPTER 4. THE COMPLEXITY OF BECOMING A TEACHER IN UNIVERSITY, SCHOOL, AND CLASSROOM CONTEXTS

Blogs

Haynes, K. (2013, March). How to mentor a student teacher.

Consider sharing this blog with mentor teachers and with student teachers. Discuss the information presented and generate additional ideas that could help the mentoring process and troubleshoot potential conflicts.

www.teachhub.com/how-mentor-student-teacher

WeAreTeachers Staff. (2015, February 27). How to be (or find) a truly great teaching mentor.

Use tips from this blog when working with teacher candidates, student teachers, novice teachers, and mentors. Discuss the symbiotic relationship from the mentoring experience because it is a form of professional development for everyone involved. What are other tips you can add to this?

www.weareteachers.com/how-to-be-or-find-a-truly-great-teaching-mentor/

Videos

Connell, G. (2013, December 19). *Teacher tips for student teachers: Veteran teachers give their best pieces of advice for student teachers.*

Consider using this video in class with teacher candidates and student teachers. Seasoned teachers share advice and tips for student teachers. Ask them which points they have heard already and which ideas they will work on for this semester. You could use this video with mentor teachers to see if they have anything to add. Perhaps they could make their own videos.

https://www.scholastic.com/teachers/blog-posts/genia-connell/teachers-share-our-best-tips-student-teachers/
Note: Scroll down the post to find the video.

Randazzo, L. (2018, June 23). *High school teacher vlog: advice for student teachers from a mentor teacher.*

Consider using this video and others like it to stimulate class discussion on what to expect and how to prepare for student teaching. Ask candidates to make a list of the points that stood out to them, as well as points that they wonder about from "hearsay."

www.youtube.com/watch?v=f3N_F7ieq5s

Teaching Channel. (n.d.). *Learn ways to foster learning in an atmosphere of inclusiveness and empathy.*

While the focus of this video is on the school classroom setting, consider how the same message applies in teacher preparation. Watch the video with candidates and ask: How can we build an atmosphere of inclusiveness and empathy with one another as teacher candidates, as student teachers, and with mentor teachers and teacher colleagues?

www.teachingchannel.org/video/empathy-community

Other Materials

ASCD. (n.d.). School culture and climate.

Review the video, articles, and other resources from links provided in this ASCD "Topic." Select items to share with your audience.

www.ascd.org/research-a-topic/school-culture-and-climate-resources.aspx#targetText=School%20culture%20refers%20to%20the,promote%20students'%20ability%20to%20learn

Australian Institute for Teaching and School Leadership. (n.d.). *How do I engage in classroom observation?*

Consider using this PowerPoint presentation (in PDF form) to promote classroom observation as a way to encourage reflection and growth in teaching. This can be implemented with teachers at all levels, including teacher candidates, student teachers, novices, and mentors.

www.aitsl.edu.au/docs/default-source/default-document-library/11-how-do-i-engage-in-classroom-observation-04788f91b1e86477b58fff00006709da.pdf

CHAPTER 5. CONNECTING COURSEWORK TO INSTRUCTION

Blogs

Burns, M. (2016, January 18). Mid-year reflection: Setting PD goals.

Use information from this blog to discuss goal setting in teaching. Discussion points could include: How can we set short-term and long-range goals? How can we monitor our progress toward reaching those goals? How often should we revisit our goals? How do we revise our goals?

www.edutopia.org/blog/mid-year-reflection-setting-pd-goals-monica-burns

Foltos, L. (2018, January 29). Teachers learn better together.

Consider using this blog to discuss ways that teachers use collaboration as professional development. When teachers plan and reflect together, their students benefit. Think about reviewing the ideas from this blog to stimulate more ideas about how teachers can foster a culture of collaboration that starts in the teacher candidate phase of the teaching journey.

www.edutopia.org/article/teachers-learn-better-together

Videos

Edutopia. (2018, November 16). *How learning happens.*

While this series of 14 videos focuses on classrooms, make connections to how the content is also true for teacher candidates in coursework and field experiences, student teachers, novice teachers, and mentor teachers.

www.edutopia.org/how-learning-happens

EL Education. (n.d.). *Students own their progress.*

See how one school empowers their students with goal setting. Discuss how learning to teach also requires goal setting and monitoring our own progress of teaching methods. Lead an activity where teacher candidates, student teachers, and/or novice teachers consider how they want to grow in teaching and show them how to make realistic, specific goals that they can monitor.

eleducation.org/resources/students-own-their-progress

TEDx. (2016, November). *How to get better at the things you care about | Eduardo Briceño | TEDxManhattanBeach.*

Consider sharing this TED Talk and then leading a discussion about the implications for teachers. How can we get better at teaching, regardless of where we are in our career?

www.ted.com/talks/eduardo_briceno_how_to_get_better_at_the_things_you_care_about#t-24062

CHAPTER 6. NEGOTIATING CLASSROOM COMPLEXITY

Books

Amazon.com. (n.d.) "Classroom routines" [Search].

Peruse this list of books on establishing classroom routines. Provide choices in readings and provide time for student teachers, novice teachers, or mentor teachers to share what they learned from the books and how they tried the ideas in their classrooms.

amzn.to/2I26RoW

Dweck, C. S. (2016). *Mindset: The new psychology of success.* New York, NY: Ballantine Books.

Consider using this book as a required reading and/or as a professional resource (along with the resources that follow) to assist with planning class lecture notes and discussion points related to growth mindset. Discuss salient points with your teacher candidates, student teachers, novice teachers, and mentor teachers.

amzn.to/2NDE4LB

Article

Karkouti, I. M., Wolsey, T. D., & Toprak, M. (2019, September 13). Restoring hope for Syrian refugees: Social support students need to excel at school. *International Migration*. Advance online publication. doi: 10.1111/imig.12642

Teachers at all levels of experience encounter students with varying needs. This article explores how social support helps students succeed in school and how the lack of such support may be detrimental.

Other Materials

Mindset Works, Inc. (2017). *Mindset works* [Website].

Review the tools available on these websites about mindset. How can you use these tools to discuss growth mindset in becoming a metacognitive teacher? How can you use these tools to help teachers of all stages consider how they foster growth mindset in their classrooms?

www.mindsetworks.com/

CHAPTER 7. YOUR TEACHING JOURNEY

Blogs

Heggart, K. (2015, February 4). Developing a growth mindset in teachers and staff.

Read this blog and consider how you can use the information with your teacher candidates, novice teachers, and mentor teachers.

www.edutopia.org/discussion/developing-growth-mindset-teachers-and-staff

Wolpert-Gawron, H. (2019, August 14). Learning your way toward wellness.

Use this short post to stimulate discussion about how teachers at all stages can continue their own learning about life beyond the school walls. Ask teachers to make a list of things they want to learn about this year, such as starting a new hobby or exploring local museums.

neatoday.org/2019/08/14/tips-for-teacher-wellness/

Other Materials

Australian Institute for Teaching and School Leadership. (2017). *Build a professional growth culture.*

The information on professional development on the AITSL website is relevant for teachers at all stages of their careers. Resources relate to performance and development, reflection and goal setting, professional practice and learning, and feedback, reflection, and review. Within each area you will find power points, guides, videos, and other resources.

www.aitsl.edu.au/lead-develop/develop-others/build-a-professional-growth-culture

Australian Institute for Teaching and School Leadership. (2017). *Great teachers never stop learning.*

Consider using resources on improving practice from the AITSL website to promote teachers' reflection on their professional growth. Videos are included, along with hundreds of other resources.

www.aitsl.edu.au/teach/improve-practice

Gerstein, J. (2014, August 29). *The Educator with a Growth Mindset: A professional development workshop.*

Review this professional development workshop and use it or use ideas presented to help you create your own presentation and professional development with teacher candidates, novice teachers, and mentor teachers.

usergeneratededucation.wordpress.com/2014/08/29/the-educator-with-a-growth-mindset-a-staff-workshop/

Glossary

Depending on your state or province and your school district, the vocabulary that teachers and administrators use may vary a bit. We used the following terms and definitions in this book, but you should know that sometimes a term may have a similar or even identical meaning as another used in your school.

Adaptations: Changes made to lessons.

Assessments: Techniques used to determine students' learning.

Coaching: Guidance by educators to improve teaching and learning.

Common Core Standards: National standards for English Language Arts (ELA) and Math. Some states require Common Core standards instead of their own ELA and Math standards.

Cooperating Teacher (also called *Mentor Teacher* or *Master Teacher*): The teacher hosting candidates for field experiences and student teachers.

Context: Your teaching and/or learning location.

Coursework: Classes taken to prepare for teaching.

Curriculum: Subject-area content taught using guiding documents (e.g., teacher manuals).

Differentiated Instruction: Tailored instruction to meet students' learning needs. This is often accomplished in small groups.

Evidence-based: Grounded in research evidence.

Fidelity: Faithful adherence to a program.

Field Experience (also called *Internship* or *Practicum*): Time spent in schools connected to coursework.

Growth Mindset: Believing that you can do something through effort and persistence.

International Literacy Association (ILA) Standards for the Preparation of Literacy Professionals: Literacy-specific professional aims for teachers at all levels.

Inservice Teachers: Teachers who are currently engaged in the profession.

Instructional Coach: Educators who work with teachers instead of with students. These teacher-leaders provide assistance to teachers of all experience levels to improve teaching and learning.

Intentional: Consciously deliberate.

Interns: Teacher candidates in field experiences accompanying coursework (prior to full-time student teaching).

Internships: Field experiences that accompany coursework.

Longitudinal Research: An investigation spanning years.

Master Teacher (also called *Cooperating Teacher* or *Mentor Teacher*): A teacher who hosts candidates for field experiences and student teachers or serves as a mentor for new teachers.

Mentor Teacher (also called *Cooperating Teacher* or *Master Teacher*): A teacher who hosts student teachers or serves as a mentor for new teachers.

Metacognition: Consciously thinking about your thinking.

Metacognitive Teaching: Continuously reflecting on and monitoring teaching practices while making adaptations as needed.

Novice Teacher: First-year or beginning teacher.

Pedagogy: Knowledge of teaching methods; the science of teaching; instructional methods used to teach; how to teach.

Pedagogical Content Knowledge: Deep understanding of how to teach particular content.

Practicum: Field experience connected with coursework.

Prerequisite: Requirement before something can happen.

Reflection: Thinking about what happened and what might be changed for next time.

Self-Care: Taking time to nurture your mental and physical well-being.

Scaffolding: Structured assistance to build success.

State Standards: Specific requirements by grade levels and content areas set by the state. Some states require Common Core standards instead of their own ELA and Math standards.

Student Teaching: Full-time teaching while still a university student. This usually occurs in the last semester before graduation.

Teacher Candidate: University student who is taking coursework in hopes of being a teacher; teacher education major.

Teacher Preparation Program: University program that is dedicated to preparing future teachers.

Trajectory: Pathway toward a specific goal, such as becoming a metacognitive teacher.

University Supervisor: Someone from a teacher preparation program who observes and provides guidance to a candidate or student teacher. This person also communicates with the cooperating (mentor) teacher.

Vision: Your purpose for teaching.

References

Beck, C., & Kosnik, C. (2017). The continuum of pre-service and in-service teacher education. In D. J. Clandinin & J. Husu (Eds.), *The SAGE handbook of research on teacher education* (pp. 107–122). Thousand Oaks, CA: Sage.

Billick, I., & Case, T. (1994). Higher order interactions in ecological communities: What are they and how can they be detected? *Ecology, 75*(6), 1530–1543. doi:10.2307/1939614

Boushey, G., & Moser, J. (2014). *The Daily 5: Fostering literacy independence in the elementary grades* (2nd ed.). Portland, ME: Stenhouse.

Braaten, M. (2019). Persistence of the two-worlds pitfall: Learning to teach within and across settings. *Science Education, 103*(1), 61–91.

Bullock, S. M. (2011). *Inside teacher education: Challenging prior views of teaching and learning*. Boston, MA: Sense.

Cornish, L., & Jenkins, K. A. (2012). Encouraging teacher development through embedding reflective practice in assessment. *Asia–Pacific Journal of Teacher Education, 40*(2), 159–170. https://doi.org/10.1080/1359866X.2012.669825

Daniels, H. (2002). *Literature circles: Voice and choice in book clubs and reading* groups (2nd ed.). Portland, ME: Stenhouse.

Darling-Hammond, L. (2006). *Powerful teacher education: Lessons from exemplary programs*. San Francisco, CA: Jossey-Bass.

Duffy, G. G. (2005). Developing metacognitive teachers: Visioning and the expert's changing role in teacher education and professional development. In S. E. Israel, C. C. Block, K. L. Bauserman, & K. Kinnucan-Welsch (Eds.), *Metacognition in literacy learning: Theory, assessment, instruction, and professional development* (pp. 299–314). Mahwah, NJ: Lawrence Erlbaum.

Duffy, G. G. (2014). *Explaining reading: A resource for explicit teaching of the Common Core Standards* (3rd ed.). New York, NY: Guilford Press.

Ehri, L. C. (1994). Development of the ability to read words: Update. In R. Ruddell, M. Ruddell, & H. Singer (Eds.), *Theoretical models and processes of reading.* (4th ed., pp. 323–358). Newark, DE: International Reading Association.

Engeström, Y. (2015). *Learning by expanding: An activity-theoretical approach to developmental research* (2nd ed.). Cambridge, United Kingdom: Cambridge University Press.

Feiman-Nemser, S. (2008). Teacher learning: How do teachers learn to teach? In M. Cochran-Smith, S. Feiman-Nemser, D. J. McIntyre, & K. E. Demers (Eds.), *Handbook of research on teacher education: Enduring questions in changing contexts* (3rd ed., pp. 699–705). New York, NY: Routledge.

Feiman-Nemser, S., & Buchmann, M. (1985). Pitfalls of experience in teacher preparation. *Teachers College Record, 87*(1), 53–65.

Goodman, Y. M. (1985). Kidwatching: Observing children in the classroom. In A. Jagger & M. T. Smith-Burke (Eds.), *Observing the language learner* (pp. 9–18). Urbana: National Council of Teachers of English & International Reading Association.

Grant, H., & Dweck, C. S. (2003). Clarifying achievement goals and their impact. *Journal of Personality and Social Psychology, 85*(3), 541–553. https://doi.org/10.1037/0022-3514.85.3.541

Griffith, R. (2017). Preservice teachers' in-the-moment teaching decisions in reading. *Literacy, 51*(1), 3–10. https://doi.org/10.1111/lit.12097

Guthrie, J. T., & Barber, A. T. (2019). Best practices for motivating students to read. In L. M. Morrow & L. B. Gambrell (Eds.), *Best practices in literacy instruction* (6th ed., pp. 52–72). New York, NY: Guilford Press.

Guthrie, J. T., & Humenick, N. M. (2004). Motivating students to read: Evidence for classroom practices that increase reading motivation and achievement. In P. McCardle & V. Chhabra (Eds.), *The voice of evidence in reading research* (pp. 329–354). Baltimore, MD: Paul H. Brookes.

Hegji, A. (2017). *An Overview of Accreditation of Higher Education in the United States.* Washington, DC: Congressional Research Service.

Henkel, C. (2019, February 4). Monday numbers—A closer look at teacher turnover in North Carolina. Retrieved from www.ncpolicywatch.com/2019/02/04/monday-numbers-a-closer-look-at-teacher-turnover-in-north-carolina/

Ingersoll, R. M., Merrill, E., Stuckey, D., & Collins, G. (2018). Seven trends: The transformation of the teaching force—Updated October 2018. *CPRE Research Reports.* Retrieved from repository.upenn.edu/cpre_researchreports/108

International Literacy Association (ILA). (2017). *Standards for the preparation of literacy professionals 2017.* Available at www.literacyworldwide.org/get-resources/standards/standards-2017

Koedinger, K. R., Booth, J. L., & Klahr, D. (2013). Instructional complexity and the science to constrain it. *Science, 342*(6161), 935–937.

Lenski, S., Ganske, K., Chambers, S., Wold, L., Dobler, E., Grisham, D. L., . . . Young, J. (2013). Literacy course priorities and signature aspects of nine elementary initial licensure programs. *Literacy Research and Instruction, 52*(1), 1–27. doi: 10.1080/19388071.2012.738778

Malloy, J. A., Marinak, B. A., & Gambrell, L. B. (2019). Evidence-based best practices for developing literate communities. In L. M. Morrow & L. B. Gambrell (Eds.), *Best practices in literacy instruction* (6th ed., pp. 3–26). New York, NY: Guilford Press.

O'Connor, K. (2018). *How to grade for learning: Linking grades to standards* (4th ed.). Thousand Oaks, CA: Sage.

Parsons, S. A., Vaughn, M., Malloy, J. A., & Pierczynski, M. (2017). The development of teachers' visions from preservice to their first years teaching: A longitudinal study. *Teaching and Teacher Education, 64*, 12–25. doi:10.1016/j.tate.2017.01.018

Pressley, M. (2005). Metacognition in literacy learning: Then, now, and in the future. In S. C. Israel, C. C. Block, K. L. Bauserman, & K. Kinnucan-Welsch (Eds.), *Metacognition in literacy learning: Theory, assessment, instruction, and professional development* (pp. 391–411). Mahwah, NJ: Lawrence Erlbaum.

Purcell-Gates, V., Duke, N. K., & Martineau, J. A. (2007). Learning to read and write genre-specific text: Roles of authentic experience and explicit teaching. *Reading Research Quarterly, 42*(1), 8–35.

Rich, B. R. (1995). Clarence Leonard (Kelly) Johnson. In National Academy of Sciences (Ed.), *Biographical Memoirs: V. 67*. Washington, DC: The National Academies Press. https://doi.org/10.17226/4894

Risko, V. J., Roskos, K., & Vukelich, C. (2005). Reflection and the self-analytic turn of mind: Toward more robust instruction in teacher education. In S. E. Israel, C. C. Block, K. L. Bauserman, & K. Kinnucan-Welsch (Eds.), *Metacognition in literacy learning: Theory, assessment, instruction, and professional development* (pp. 315–333). Mahwah, NJ: Lawrence Erlbaum.

Romer, T. A. (2003). Learning process and professional content in the theory of Donald Schön. *Reflective Practice, 4*(1), 85–93.

Roser, N. L. (2001). A place for everything and literature in its place. *The New Advocate, 14*(3), 211–221.

Scales, R. Q., Wolsey, T. D., Lenski, S., Smetana, L., Yoder, K. K., Dobler, E., . . . Young, J. (2018). Are we preparing or training teachers?: Developing professional judgment in and beyond teacher preparation programs. *Journal of Teacher Education, 69*(1), 7–21. doi:10.1177/0022487117702584

Scales, R. Q., Wolsey, T. D., Young, J., Smetana, L., Grisham, D. L., Lenski, S., . . . Chambers, S. A. (2017). Mediating factors in literacy instruction: How novice elementary teachers navigate new teaching contexts. *Reading Psychology, 38*(6), 604–651. doi:10.1080/02702711.2017.1323056

Schön, D. (1983). *The reflective practitioner: How professionals think in action.* New York, NY: Basic Books.

Serafini, F. (2011). When bad things happen to good books. *The Reading Teacher, 65*(4), 238–241. doi:10.1002/TRTR.01039

Snow, C. E., Griffin, P., & Burns, M. S. (2005). *Knowledge to support the teaching of reading: Preparing teachers for a changing world.* San Francisco, CA: Jossey-Bass.

Spiro, R. J., Coulson, R. L., Feltovich, P. J., & Anderson, D. K. (2004). Cognitive flexibility theory: Advanced knowledge acquisition in ill-structured domains. In R. B. Ruddell, & N. Unrau (Eds.), *Theoretical models and processes of reading* (5th ed., pp. 640–653). Newark, DE: International Reading Association.

Spiro, R. J., Feltovich, P. J., & Coulson, R. L. (1996). Two epistemic world-views: Prefigurative schemas and learning in complex domains. *Applied Cognitive Psychology, 10*, 51–61.

Spiro, R. J., Vispoel, W. L., Schmitz, J. G., Samarapungavan, A., & Boerger, A. E. (1987). Knowledge acquisition for application: Cognitive flexibility and transfer in complex content domains. In B. K. Britton & S. M. Glynn (Eds.), *Executive control processes in reading* (pp. 177–199). Hillsdale, NJ: Lawrence Erlbaum.

Stiggins, R. (2005). *Student-involved assessment for learning* (4th ed.). Upper Saddle River, NJ: Pearson.

Sutcher, L., Darling-Hammond, L., & Carver-Thomas, D. (2016). *A coming crisis in teaching? Teacher supply, demand, and shortages in the U.S.* Palo Alto, CA: Learning Policy Institute.

Vaughn, M., Parsons, S. A., Gallagher, M., & Branen, J. (2016). Teachers' adaptive instruction supporting students' literacy learning. *The Reading Teacher, 69*(5), 539–547. doi:10.1002/trtr.1426

Will, M. (2019, May 14). How can teachers bounce back from failure? [blog post]. *Education Week*. Retrieved from www.edweek.org/ew/articles/2019/05/15/how-can-teachers-bounce-back-from-failure.html

Wolsey, T. D., Lenski, S., & Grisham, D. L. (2020). *Assessment literacy: An educator's guide to understanding assessment, K–12*. New York, NY: Guilford Press.

Young, J. R., Scales, R. Q., Grisham, D. L., Dobler, E., Wolsey, T. D., Smetana, L., . . . Yoder, K. K. (2017). Student teachers' preparation in literacy: Cooking in someone else's kitchen. *Teacher Education Quarterly, 44*(4), 74–97.

Index

About the Authors

Roya Q. Scales, PhD, is a professor of Literacy Education at Western Carolina University in Cullowhee, NC. An educator for more than 20 years (11 as a K–2 classroom teacher), she is noted for her research on thoughtfully adaptive teaching, enactment of teachers' visions, literacy teacher education, and effective teaching of literacy. Roya served as the Program Coordinator in the B.S.Ed. and M.A.Ed. Elementary Education and Middle Grades Education Programs for 5 years. She is currently Associate Editor for *Reading & Writing Quarterly: Overcoming Learning Difficulties*. Contact Roya via email at rqscales@wcu.edu.

Thomas DeVere Wolsey, EdD, teaches graduate courses in research and literacy at the American University in Cairo and conducts professional development for teachers in Guatemala, Mexico, China, and in the United States, including the Hopi Reservation. After nearly 20 years in the classroom, mainly as an English teacher, he came to appreciate the value of narrative. Like his coauthors, he was captivated by the participating teachers' narratives, which provided rich data and spoke directly to the essential characteristics of teaching. Contact DeVere via email at thomas.wolsey@aucegypt.edu.

Seth A. Parsons, PhD, is an associate professor in the School of Education and the Sturtevant Center for Literacy at George Mason University in Fairfax, VA. He teaches courses in the Elementary Education, Literacy, and Research Methods programs. His research focuses on teachers' adaptive instructional moves, student motivation and engagement, and teacher preparation. He is currently president of the Association of Literacy Educators and Researchers and coeditor of the journal *School–University Partnerships*. Seth leads the research efforts as a member on the Council of Directors for The National Center for Clinical Practice in Educator Preparation. Contact Seth via email at sparson5@gmu.edu.